CHERRY BOMBE

THE COOKBOOK

CHERRY
BOMBE

THE COOKBOOK

RECIPES AND STORIES FROM
100 OF THE MOST CREATIVE AND
INSPIRING WOMEN IN FOOD TODAY

Kerry Diamond and Claudia Wu
photographs by Alpha Smoot   food styling by Claudia Ficca

CLARKSON POTTER/PUBLISHERS
New York

Library of Congress Cataloguing-in-Publication Data
NAMES: Diamond, Kerry, editor. | Wu, Claudia, editor.
TITLE: *Cherry Bombe: The Cookbook* / [compiled by] Kerry Diamond and Claudia Wu;
photographs by Alpha Smoot.
DESCRIPTION: First edition. | New York : Clarkson Potter/Publishers, [2017] |
Selection of recipes from noted food writers from the editors
of the biannual *Cherry Bombe*. | Includes index.
IDENTIFIERS: LCCN 2016044131 | ISBN 9780553459524 (hardcover) |
ISBN 9780553459531 (eISBN)
SUBJECTS: LCSH: Cooking. | LCGFT: Cookbooks.
CLASSIFICATION: LCC TX714.C466675 2017 | DDC 641.5/63—dc23 LC
record available at https://lccn.loc.gov/2016044131

ISBN 978-0-553-45952-4
Ebook ISBN 978-0-553-45953-1

Printed in China
10 9 8 7 6

FOOD STYLIST: Claudia Ficca
FOOD STYLIST (PAGES 67, 159, 205, 207 & 241): Diana Yen
PROP STYLIST: Katja Greeff
BOOK & COVER DESIGN: Claudia Wu

First Edition

This book is dedicated to April Bloomfield,
Leah Chase, Cecilia Chiang, Dominique Crenn,
Ina Garten, Suzanne Goin, Dorie Greenspan,
Gabrielle Hamilton, Madhur Jaffrey, Judith Jones,
Nigella Lawson, Barbara Lynch, Ruth Reichl,
Mimi Sheraton, Nancy Silverton, Martha Stewart,
and Alice Waters.

Thank you for being domestic goddesses,
culinary trailblazers, and queens of the kitchen!

CONTENTS

INTRODUCTION

What makes a recipe special and truly worth your time? For us, it comes down to the person behind the recipe. Why cook any old dish from some anonymous recipe online when you can make one from a person you love or admire? We prefer a recipe that's the equivalent of a sweater borrowed from a girlfriend, a dog-eared book your sister lent you, or the weird knickknack that belonged to your grandmother. Dependable, interesting, nostalgia inducing, maybe even a little quirky.

That is the premise behind *Cherry Bombe: The Cookbook*. We wanted to produce a collection of meaningful, intriguing, and delicious recipes from the women who inspire us, so we emailed chefs we love, past *Cherry Bombe* cover girls and subjects, friends, and even a few strangers and asked for a recipe they treasure.

Once the submissions started pouring in, the *Cherry Bombe* team started cooking. We tested everything ourselves in our small New York City apartments. We wanted to vouch for every dish in this book and ensure that anyone, at any skill level, and with any kind of kitchen setup, could make all the recipes. We visited our local grocery stores and bodegas more times than we thought humanly possible and we cooked through multiple heat waves. Some recipes were perfect on the first try; others took three, four, even five times to get just right. We washed a lot of dishes, composted a lot of fruit and veggie scraps, and offered a lot of food to our neighbors.

What we loved as much as the beautiful dishes were the anecdotes that each woman shared. Because of their stories, you can't help but feel their presence guiding you and cheering you on as you work your way through the cookbook. As you chop, blend, beat, and sauté, you'll realize there's girl power swirling all around you. The late author Laurie Colwin—whose much-loved books *Home Cooking* and *More Home Cooking* were big influences on this project—said it best: "No one who cooks cooks alone. Even at her most solitary, a cook in the kitchen is surrounded by generations of cooks past, the advice and menus of cooks present, the wisdom of cookbook writers."

Thank you to all the wonder(ful) women who contributed recipes to this project. There are so many different talents in this cookbook, from pastry chefs, food stylists, and bakers to editors, bloggers, and farmers. *Cherry Bombe* was created to celebrate women in the world of food and we're thrilled to continue our mission here. Lastly, thank *you* for bringing these recipes to life. Happy cooking.

YOU'RE THE BOMBE!

Kerry
+
Claudia

CONTRIBUTORS

MASHAMA BAILEY • KATIE BALDWIN • CAMILLE BECERRA • EMMA BENGTSSON • KATE BRASHARES • JENI BRITTON BAUER • KATIE BUTTON • GABRIELA CÁMARA • SUE S. CHAN • DANIELLE CHANG • AMY CHAPLIN • ADRIENNE CHEATHAM • ERIKA CHOU • ASHLEY CHRISTENSEN • MELISSA CLARK • NINA CLEMENTE • AMANDA COHEN • LOUISA CONRAD • CHLOE COSCARELLI • JUSTINE D. • CASSIDEE DABNEY • HOMA DASHTAKI • ANGELA DIMAYUGA • LISA DONOVAN • CHARLOTTE DRUCKMAN • MELANIE DUNEA • EMILY ELSEN • MELISSA ELSEN • RENEE ERICKSON • ERIN FAIRBANKS • ANYA FERNALD • LAURA FERRARA • LISA Q. FETTERMAN • CLAUDIA FICCA • CAITLIN FREEMAN • SARAH GAVIGAN • ANDREA GENTL • YANA GILBUENA • LAILA GOHAR • BERTHA GONZÁLEZ NIEVES • ARAN GOYOAGA • VICTORIA GRANOF • AMY GUITTARD • CHRISTINA HA • HAWA HASSAN • TANYA HOLLAND • MARTHA HOOVER • VIVIAN HOWARD • SARAH HYMANSON

• AMIRAH KASSEM • SOHUI KIM • EVAN KLEIMAN • KARLIE KLOSS • AMANDA KLUDT • ELISE KORNACK • DANIELLE KOSANN • LAURA KOSANN • JESSICA KOSLOW • SARA KRAMER • PRIYA KRISHNA • AGATHA KULAGA • PADMA LAKSHMI • YVETTE LEEPER-BUENO • KAREN LEIBOWITZ • JENN LOUIS • JAMIE MALONE • MELIA MARDEN • KATRINA MARKOFF • ERIN MCKENNA • AMANDA MERROW • KLANCY MILLER • PREETI MISTRY • NILOU MOTAMED • KRISTY MUCCI • CHRISTINE MUHLKE • ERIN PATINKIN • LEAH PENNIMAN • NAOMI POMEROY • NICOLE PONSECA • ELISABETH PRUEITT • CAROLINE RANDALL WILLIAMS • ILIANA REGAN • ANDREA REUSING • DOMINICA RICE-CISNEROS • JESSAMYN RODRIGUEZ • JENNIFER RUBELL • AVERY RUZICKA • NAZ SAHIN OZCAN • JORDAN SALCITO • ANNE SAXELBY • JULIA SHERMAN • GAIL SIMMONS • LEXIE SMITH • NAOMI STARKMAN • MINA STONE • HEIDI SWANSON • CHRISSY TEIGEN • SIERRA TISHGART • CHRISTINA TOSI • ALISSA WAGNER • ANNA WEINBERG • ELETTRA WIEDEMANN • JOY WILSON • MOLLY YEH • DIANA YEN

TOOLS & RULES

Our Favorite Tools

Here are the kitchen essentials we use again and again.

Cutting board: Buy a large sturdy one. A small cutting board won't do the job.

Knives: You don't need an entire set. You can accomplish a lot with a large chef's knife and a paring knife. Just make sure to keep them sharp.

Colander: A must for draining pasta, washing berries, and making ricotta. We also use ours to store fruits and vegetables in the fridge and on the counter.

Sauté pan: You'll find a million uses for this, from scrambling eggs to toasting nuts to warming up leftovers.

Stockpot: Get one that's large and lidded. Lift it before you buy it to make sure it feels sturdy in your hands and not too heavy.

Baking sheets: Ours are constantly in use. Buy two identical ones so they can nest and not take up extra storage space.

Wooden spoon: Sometimes the simplest tools are best. A beautiful handcrafted spoon will make a great heirloom one day, so choose well and take care of it.

Flat spatula: This keeps things neat and intact when we need to move hot food.

Box grater: Buy a quality one that won't slip around your counter and use it to grate cheese, chocolate, veggies, even fresh tomatoes.

Measuring cups and spoons: A well-made set can last a lifetime.

Mixing bowls: Buy a set of nesting bowls in a color you love since you'll use them—and see them—all the time.

Kerry's Extras

Microplane: I reach for this when I need to finely grate something—nutmeg, lemon zest, Parmesan. It's super precise, so you feel like a chef when you use it.

Clip-on thermometer: This can make the difference between a kitchen fail and a big success.

Vitamix blender: A pricey purchase, yes, but if you use your blender a lot, it's a worthwhile investment.

Dutch oven: I feel like I'm channeling Julia Child every time I use mine.

Ramekins: Use these to make individual baked items, organize your mise en place, or portion out snacks.

Claudia's Extras

Mandoline: I have the Japanese kind, which is inexpensive, compact, and easy to store.

Kitchen scale: Pastry chefs and bakers love scales because they're more exact than measuring cups and spoons.

Mini food processor: I use mine to make hummus, quick sorbets, and sauces, and it takes up way less space than a full-size one.

Handheld mixer: Speaking of space, if there's no room on your counter for a stand mixer, a handheld model will get the job done.

Cookie scoop: Do you bake a lot of cookies? They'll never look more professional and uniform than when you portion the dough with this tool.

Bombe Squad Kitchen Rules

1. Read recipes all the way through and plan your grocery list with specific quantities. It's a bummer to have to run *back* to the grocery store after you've started cooking.

2. Don't start cooking until your space is organized and your ingredients are lined up. It will make your kitchen time more enjoyable, productive, and safe. And clean as you go. You'll thank us later.

3. Plan your music or podcast lineup before you get your hands dirty. You don't want to be skipping around your playlist with flour-covered fingers.

4. It's fine to look cute in the kitchen, but don't sacrifice safety or hygiene. Put your hair back so it doesn't get in the food, protect your clothes with an apron, and wear shoes in case you drop something on those toes of yours.

5. No dull knives allowed. Get what's called a honing steel and learn how to take care of your knives. If you've never used a steel before, it's easier than you think.

6. Use the timer on your oven or phone to track when things are done, especially if you're multitasking. At the same time, learn to trust your instincts and use all of your senses—not just your sense of taste. You often can tell if something is ready by how it smells, looks, or sounds.

7. Safety first. Be careful around anything hot, splattering, and sharp! If your smoke alarm goes off while you're cooking and you remove the batteries, don't forget to put them back in.

8. We love a good food photo. Snap some pictures as you cook for a visual diary of your creations. And don't be afraid to share them.

9. When friends ask if they can help in the kitchen, don't be modest or coy. Say yes, especially when they ask if they can help with the dishes.

10. Kitchen fail? Don't fret. That's why the universe created pizza.

GROCERIES:

EGGS
BUTTER
ALMOND MILK
ROSÉ
CAT FOOD!
PARCHMENT PAPER
KOMBUCHA
CHEESECLOTH
CHOCOLATE
~~SRIRACHA~~
CILANTRO
COCONUT OIL
ARROWROOT?
TAHINI
FLOWERS

MAINS

BEET RICOTTA DUMPLINGS
WITH BROWNED BUTTER & SAGE

Evan Kleiman

These pillowy dumplings, topped with butter, sage, and a soft shower of grated Parmesan, taste earthy and ethereal at the same time. The host of the popular *Good Food* program on Los Angeles public radio station KCRW, Evan first discovered gnocchi made with ricotta years ago in Rome and was blown away. This dish is her tribute to that taste memory. The key to these gnocchi is using the freshest beets you can find, which add color and flavor, as well as basket ricotta, a dense type of ricotta that has been drained of extra liquid and contributes to the fluffy texture.

Makes 4 servings

½ pound red beets (3 or 4 small beets)
1 pound basket ricotta (see Tip)
1 large egg
1 cup grated Parmigiano-Reggiano cheese, plus more for serving
¼ teaspoon kosher salt
Freshly ground black pepper
1 cup all-purpose flour, plus more for dredging
½ cup (1 stick) unsalted butter
¼ cup fresh sage leaves

Preheat the oven to 450°F.

Wrap the beets in aluminum foil and place them on a rimmed baking sheet. Bake until fork-tender, about 45 minutes. Remove from the oven, open the foil, and let the beets cool. Peel the beets and cut into 1-inch pieces. Transfer the beets to a food processor and purée.

Transfer ¾ cup of the beet purée to a large bowl and add the ricotta, egg, Parmigiano-Reggiano, salt, and some pepper. If you have extra beet purée, reserve it for another use. Mix well with a wooden spoon. Slowly stir in the flour, then stir until the dough just comes together. Cover and refrigerate for 2 hours or up to overnight.

Line a baking sheet with parchment paper and lightly dust the parchment with flour. Heavily dust your work surface with flour. Drop a walnut-size piece of the dough in the flour, coat all sides, then roll the dough around with your palms to form a small ball. Set the dumpling on the prepared baking sheet and repeat until you have used all the dough. Place the sheet of prepared gnocchi in the refrigerator for 1 hour to firm up. The gnocchi can be formed up to 1 day ahead.

Heat a sauté pan over medium-high heat, add the butter, and let it melt without moving the pan. When the butter has begun to brown around the edges, pick up the sauté pan and swirl to keep the melted butter from burning. Add the sage leaves and reduce the heat to medium. Cook until the sage is crispy, 1 to 2 minutes. Remove from the heat and set aside.

Bring a large pot of salted water to a gentle simmer over medium heat. Lift the piece of parchment off the baking sheet and slip the dumplings into the water. Cook until the dumplings float to the surface, 2 to 3 minutes, then cook for 1 minute more, until the dumplings are firm but tender. Using a slotted spoon, remove the dumplings from the water and place on a serving platter. Top with the browned butter and sage, sprinkle with Parmigiano-Reggiano, and serve immediately.

Tip: If you can't find basket ricotta, you can make your own. Put traditional ricotta in a sieve or a cheesecloth-lined colander set over a bowl. Cover with plastic wrap or a dishtowel and refrigerate for 8 hours or up to overnight.

MANICOTTI
WITH CHERRY TOMATO SAUCE

Sarah Gavigan

While manicotti made with pasta sheets can be a belly bomb, Sarah's classic version made with crepes is surprisingly light—a good thing, since you'll want seconds. Instead of traditional "red sauce," she uses cherry tomato sauce, which contributes to the brightness of the dish, as do the fresh herbs in the ricotta. Even though Sarah's chef adventures have been very cross-cultural, this Nashville restaurateur, who owns the eateries Otaku, POP, and Little Octopus, grew up in an Italian-American household where dishes such as this one were customary fare. Her manicotti is a fun recipe to make with friends, as they can stuff the crepes as you work the skillet.

Makes about 20 crepes (5 servings)

Sauce
2 quarts Sicilian cherry tomato sauce (see Tip)
Kosher salt and freshly ground black pepper

Cheese Filling
28 ounces ricotta cheese
2 large eggs
1 cup finely chopped fresh flat-leaf parsley
1 cup finely chopped fresh mint
1 teaspoon freshly grated nutmeg
1½ cups freshly grated Pecorino Romano cheese

Crepes
4 large eggs
1 cup all-purpose flour
1 teaspoon kosher salt
2 tablespoons unsalted butter, melted

½ cup freshly grated Pecorino Romano cheese

Preheat the oven to 325°F.

Heat the sauce: Bring the tomato sauce to a simmer in a medium pot. Season with salt and pepper.

Make the cheese filling: Put the ricotta in a large bowl and mix in the eggs one at a time. Stir in the herbs, nutmeg, and Pecorino. Set the mixture aside.

Make the crepes: In a large bowl, beat the eggs with a handheld mixer until fluffy. Gradually add the flour, salt, and 1 cup water. As the batter thickens, add an additional ½ cup water and beat until smooth. The batter should stick to the spoon but be runny.

Heat a nonstick skillet over medium heat. Brush with a light layer of melted butter. Ladle 2 to 3 tablespoons of the crepe batter into the pan and swirl it around until it covers the surface. The crepe will set in less than a minute. Do not let it brown. Flip, cook the other side for a few seconds, and slide it onto a plate. Repeat with the rest of the batter, adding more butter to the pan every few crepes. (You can pile the finished crepes on top of one another; they won't stick together.)

If batter thickens while standing, mix in a splash of water.

Assemble and bake the crepes: Ladle 1 cup of the tomato sauce to cover the bottom of a glass baking dish or other large casserole. Lay one crepe on a flat surface and fill with 3 tablespoons of the cheese filling along the center. Roll the crepe like a cigar and place it in the baking dish. Repeat, placing the crepes side by side in a single layer. When finished, cover the crepes with tomato sauce and reserve any extra to serve with the baked crepes. Sprinkle with the Pecorino and bake for 45 minutes or until until browned on top.

Serve family-style with the extra sauce in a bowl on the side.

Tip: The cherry tomato sauce might require some online sleuthing to hunt down. Look for the kind made with Sicilian cherry tomatoes that comes in a pop-top bottle. The sauce is thin and mildly flavored and works nicely with this recipe.

NONNA GRAZIA'S PASTA E PISELLI
(GRANDMA'S PASTA & PEAS)

Claudia Ficca

This warm bowl of pasta shells in a light tomato-y broth is pure comfort food for Claudia, one of our favorite food stylists and part of the team that worked on this very cookbook. Claudia grew up eating this one-pot dish made by her nonna, who is in her nineties and with whom she still speaks almost every day. Nonna was raised in Calabria, Italy, where her mother and grandmother ran a farm and a vineyard and sold the fruits and vegetables they harvested. This dish originated with them and reflects the rustic fare they cooked every day.

Makes 8 servings

2 tablespoons olive oil, plus more for finishing
1 medium onion, chopped (about 1½ cups)
Kosher salt
1 cup passata (unsalted strained tomatoes)
1 pound dried shell pasta
1 (1-pound) bag frozen baby sweet peas
1 cup freshly grated Parmigiano-Reggiano cheese

Heat the olive oil in a large pot over medium heat. Add the onion and sauté until soft, about 3 minutes. Add a pinch of salt and stir.

Add the tomatoes and stir to combine. Bring to a simmer and cook, stirring occasionally, for about 3 minutes.

Stir in 7 cups water and turn the heat to high. Cover the pot and bring to a boil.

When the sauce is boiling, add 2 tablespoons of salt and the pasta. Cook, uncovered, at a gentle boil, stirring occasionally, for about 11 minutes. Stir in the peas and taste for seasoning. Cook for 2 minutes more. Turn off the heat, cover the pot, and let sit for 5 minutes.

Ladle the pasta, peas, and broth into individual bowls and drizzle with a generous amount of olive oil. Top with the grated cheese and serve.

Tip: Claudia customizes this dish with whatever ingredients she happens to have on hand. Add fresh basil leaves to the oil in the beginning or toss a Parmigiano-Reggiano rind in with the pasta while it's cooking. (Be sure to remove the leaves and/or the rind before serving.) You also can sauté a handful of chopped pancetta before adding the onion to the pan. Or, for some heat, sprinkle a teaspoon of chopped hot peppers on each serving.

SIMPLE SUMMER TOMATO SAUCE

Anya Fernald

When that happy time known as tomato season arrives, try this easy four-ingredient recipe. Anya, the CEO and cofounder of Belcampo, a sustainable meat company, uses an interesting technique she learned while working with farmers in Italy: grating tomatoes. During her time there, she marveled at the simplicity of Italian kitchens and how creatively they use the most basic of tools. They shape pasta with the tines of a fork, pound meat with rolling pins, and shred onions, tomatoes, and even garlic with cheese graters. Here, the grater makes quick work of tomatoes, turning them into pulp with little mess and little effort on your part.

Makes about 3 cups

1 small or ½ medium onion
8 ripe tomatoes (Anya loves Early Girl or Roma tomatoes)
¼ cup olive oil, plus more for serving
1 teaspoon kosher salt, plus more as needed

Using the small holes on a box grater, grate the onion into a medium bowl. Using the large holes, coarsely grate the tomatoes into a large bowl and discard the skins.

Heat the olive oil in a pan or pot large enough to hold all the tomato pulp over medium-low heat. Add the onions and cook for 10 minutes. Don't let them brown. Add the tomatoes and cook for 20 minutes more, or until the juices have reduced slightly but the sauce is still liquid. Reduce the heat to low if necessary. Add the salt, stir, and taste for seasoning.

To serve, toss the sauce with pasta and top with basil, olive oil, and cheese.

PINK SPAGHETTI
WITH BEET & RICOTTA SAUCE

Elettra Wiedemann

This beet-ricotta combo creates a luscious fuchsia-colored sauce that literally stains the pasta for a fun twist on traditional spaghetti sauce. The basil, toasted walnuts, and lemon zest that top the dish provide an earthy, fragrant counterpart to the creamy sauce and another pop of color. Leave it to Elettra, cookbook author, founder of the website *Impatient Foodie*, and a food contributor at *Refinery29*, to come up with a new Italian classic.

Makes 4 to 6 servings

Kosher salt
2 red beets, the size of tennis balls
2 tablespoons plus ¼ cup olive oil
½ cup boiling water
2 cups part-skim ricotta
1 pound dried spaghetti
¼ cup freshly grated Parmigiano-
    Reggiano cheese
½ cup chopped fresh basil
¼ cup chopped toasted walnuts
Zest of 2 lemons

Fill a large pot with water and several large pinches of salt and bring to a boil.

Peel the beets, then shred them in a food processor, using a shredding blade, or on the large holes of a box grater. You'll have about 4 cups shredded beets.

Heat 2 tablespoons of the olive oil in a medium sauté pan over medium heat. Add the grated beets and a pinch of salt and sauté, stirring frequently, for 3 to 4 minutes. Once the beets have softened, add the ½ cup boiling water and cook for 3 minutes more.

Transfer the beets to a food processor, add the remaining ¼ cup olive oil, and purée into a smooth paste. Add the ricotta and 1½ teaspoons salt. Purée again until very smooth. Set aside.

Cook the spaghetti in the pot of boiling water according to the package instructions. Reserve 1 cup of the pasta cooking water and drain the spaghetti.

In a large bowl, quickly combine the hot pasta with three-quarters of the beet-ricotta sauce and mix together well. If the sauce is too thick, add the reserved pasta water 1 tablespoon at a time. Add more sauce and/or water if necessary. Any extra sauce will keep in the refrigerator for a few days (see Tip).

Twirl a serving of pasta onto a plate or into a bowl and sprinkle with some Parmigiano-Reggiano, basil, walnuts, and lemon zest. Repeat with the remaining pasta. Serve immediately.

Tip: Use the extra pasta sauce as a veggie dip, sandwich spread, or crostini topping.

EASY CRAB ROLLS
WITH AVOCADO

Chrissy Teigen

Buttery, toasty buns stuffed with creamy crab will make you feel like you're on vacation, even when you're stuck at home. And the best part is that you can make them in five minutes or less. This super straightforward recipe can be easily doubled or even tripled if you've got a lot of friends or family to feed. That's one of Chrissy's trademarks: yummy eats meant to be enjoyed with pals, not labored over. Delicious, unfussy meals are why this cookbook author and social media superstar has such a big following for her food.

Makes 4 sandwiches

1 (8-ounce) container jumbo lump
  crabmeat, drained
1 avocado, pitted, peeled, and diced
¼ cup mayonnaise
2 tablespoons fresh lemon juice
2 tablespoons finely minced fresh
  chives, plus more for garnish
Kosher salt
2 tablespoons unsalted butter, at
  room temperature
4 hot dog buns

Preheat the broiler.

In a medium bowl, gently mix together the crab, avocado, mayo, lemon juice, and chives. Season with salt.

Butter the inside of the hot dog buns generously and put them on a baking sheet. Broil until toasty, 2 to 3 minutes. Remove from the oven. Divide the filling among the rolls, garnish with chives, and serve.

ROASTED BRANZINI
WITH TOMATOES, POTATOES & HERBS

Katie Button

For Katie, this recipe brings her back to her days at Spain's famed El Bulli restaurant—where she both launched her career and met her husband. "This is my version of a dish that you will find all over the country, with perfectly cooked fish and melt-in-your-mouth tomatoes," she says. A busy mom and the chef behind Cúrate and Nightbell in Asheville, North Carolina, Katie loves that she can whip up this family favorite with just one bowl and one pan, cutting down on dirty dishes.

Preheat the oven to 425°F.

In a large bowl, combine the potatoes, onion, garlic, ¼ cup olive oil, ½ teaspoon of salt, and some pepper. Pour the mixture onto a baking sheet in an even layer. Roast for 20 minutes.

Using the same bowl, combine the tomatoes, 1 tablespoon olive oil, 6 thyme sprigs, 4 oregano sprigs, ½ teaspoon salt, and a pinch of black pepper.

Coat each branzino with ½ tablespoon olive oil and season the inside and outside of the fish with ½ teaspoon salt and a pinch of pepper. Stuff each with 1 sprig of thyme and 1 sprig of oregano.

Remove the potatoes from the oven and pour the white wine over them. Spread the tomatoes and herbs on top of the potatoes in an even layer and return the pan to the oven for 10 minutes.

Remove the pan from the oven. Lay the branzini on top of the vegetables and roast for 20 minutes more, or until the fish is just cooked through. Transfer to a platter and serve immediately.

Makes 4 servings

1½ pounds Yukon Gold potatoes, sliced approximately ⅛ to ¼ inch thick
1 medium yellow onion, thinly sliced
4 garlic cloves, thinly sliced
¼ cup plus 2 tablespoons olive oil
Kosher salt and freshly ground black pepper
1 pound tomatoes (approximately 3 medium tomatoes), thinly sliced
8 sprigs fresh thyme
6 sprigs fresh oregano
2 whole branzino, about 1 pound each
½ cup dry white wine

SWEET & SOUR SHRIMP
WITH CHERRY TOMATOES

Padma Lakshmi

This tangy dish is bursting with so many flavors—preserved lemon, dried apricot, cumin seeds, fennel seeds, and more. Whole dried chiles add a nice warmth that radiates throughout, and of course, this being Padma's dish, you have the option of amping up the heat. The *Cherry Bombe* cover girl, *Top Chef* star, and bestselling author makes no secret of her love for all things hot and spicy. Whether in life or in cooking, the words *boring* and *bland* don't exist in her vocabulary.

In a medium bowl, toss the shrimp with the lemon juice and ¼ teaspoon of the salt. Cover and set aside.

Heat the canola oil in a deep skillet or wok over medium heat. Stir in the cumin and fennel seeds and sauté until fragrant, about 30 seconds. Toss in the shallots and bell pepper and sauté for 5 to 7 minutes more.

Add the dried chiles, garlic, and ginger to the skillet and sauté for 3 to 4 minutes more. Stir in the butter and tomatoes, reduce the heat to low, and simmer, uncovered, for 12 to 15 minutes, until the liquid has reduced by half.

Toss in the dried apricots, preserved lemon, and turmeric and simmer for 5 to 7 minutes more. Taste for seasoning and add the remaining ¼ teaspoon salt if needed.

Stir in the shrimp, coating it with the sauce. Cook, stirring once or twice, just until the shrimp becomes opaque, 3 to 4 minutes. Be careful not to overcook the shrimp. Toss in the cilantro and remove any chile tops that popped off during cooking. Serve over rice.

Makes 4 servings

1 pound large shrimp, peeled and deveined

1 tablespoon fresh lemon juice

½ teaspoon kosher salt

2 tablespoons canola oil

½ teaspoon cumin seeds

½ teaspoon fennel seeds

1 cup minced shallots

1 cup diced yellow bell pepper

2 dried red chiles, such as Kashmiri for mild heat or Thai for extra heat

1 teaspoon minced garlic

2 tablespoons minced fresh ginger

2 tablespoons unsalted butter

4 cups cherry tomatoes, halved

⅓ cup diced dried apricots

1 whole preserved lemon, seeded and diced

½ teaspoon turmeric powder

½ cup chopped fresh cilantro

Cooked rice, for serving

DUNGENESS CRAB CAKES
WITH CORN TOMATO SALSA

Renee Erickson

These decadent crab cakes feature a delicate interplay of sweet—a characteristic of West Coast Dungeness crab—and umami from the Parmesan-Dijon custard that binds everything together. The corn and tomato add brightness, both in color and flavor. This recipe is a nod to Seattle's Boat Street Cafe, where the original owner, Susan Kaplan, taught a young Renee to make a version of these crab cakes. Today, Renee is the queen of the city's food scene as chef and co-owner of The Walrus and the Carpenter and several other restaurants. A pickling fanatic, she is also the creator of Boat Street Pickles.

Make the crab cakes: In a large bowl, mix together the crab, onion, bread crumbs, brown sugar, and thyme. Set aside.

In a small bowl, lightly whisk together the egg, cream, cheese, red pepper flakes, and mustard. Carefully fold the custard into the crab mixture and refrigerate for at least 1 hour.

Preheat the oven to 400°F.

Divide the crab mixture into four equal portions. Form each into a 1¼-inch-thick patty.

Heat a large oven-safe pan over medium-high heat and add the butter. When it's bubbling, sprinkle one side of the first crab cake with cornmeal and place the cornmeal side into the butter. Repeat with the remaining crab cakes. Cook for 3 to 4 minutes. Sprinkle the naked sides with cornmeal and flip the cakes with a flat spatula, then move the pan to the oven. Bake for 10 minutes, or until the bottoms of the crab cakes are crispy.

Make the salsa: Heat the olive oil in a large frying pan over medium heat. Add the onion and sauté for 2 minutes, or until translucent. Add the cherry tomatoes and corn and sauté for another minute. Stir in the butter, lemon juice, and salt and toss until the butter is fully melted. Remove from the heat and set aside.

When ready to serve, toss the salsa with the mint and basil. Top each crab cake with some salsa.

Makes 4 servings

Crab Cakes
1 pound Dungeness or other crabmeat
3 tablespoons minced white onion
3 tablespoons bread crumbs
1 teaspoon light brown sugar
¼ teaspoon chopped fresh thyme leaves
1 large egg
⅓ cup heavy cream
1 tablespoon grated Parmigiano-Reggiano cheese
¼ teaspoon crushed red pepper flakes
1 teaspoon Dijon mustard
2 tablespoons unsalted butter
½ cup coarse cornmeal

Corn Tomato Salsa
2 teaspoons olive oil
¼ cup minced white onion
1 pint cherry tomatoes, halved
Kernels from 2 ears sweet corn
1 tablespoon unsalted butter
Juice of ½ lemon
¼ teaspoon kosher salt
1 tablespoon finely chopped fresh mint
1 tablespoon finely chopped fresh basil

SILKY EGG CUSTARD RICE
WITH LITTLENECK CLAMS

Erika Chou

This Southern Chinese dish is delicate and bright, thanks to briny clams, a splash of sesame oil, and vivid cilantro. Erika grew up eating this savory custard, as made by her mom. The restaurateur behind Northern Tiger in Manhattan, Erika opened the space to showcase the different regional cuisines that make up Chinese food, which, despite being crazy popular in the United States, is still misunderstood. "Selfishly," she says, "I want to be able to eat and share the amazing food I know and love."

Makes 1 to 2 servings

8 littleneck clams
3 large eggs
1 tablespoon light soy sauce
1 teaspoon kosher salt
1½ cups cooked white or brown rice
1 tablespoon sesame oil
1 tablespoon chopped fresh cilantro

Scrub the clams with a small brush and rinse.

In a medium bowl, beat the eggs and slowly incorporate 1 cup warm water, the soy sauce, and the salt. Fill the bottom of an 8-inch ceramic bowl with the rice, pour the egg mixture over the rice, and randomly place the clams on top.

Set a stainless steel steamer rack in a wok or large pot and add enough water to cover the bottom by an inch. Cover the pot, bring the water up to a full boil, then lower the heat to maintain a simmer. Uncover the pot and place the bowl on the rack. Cover and steam the custard for 8 to 10 minutes, or until the custard sets and the clams open.

Drizzle the dish with the sesame oil, garnish with the cilantro, and serve.

OLIVE OIL–POACHED TUNA
WITH FENNEL & ORANGES

Nina Clemente

As the chef behind L.A.'s The Smile's di Alba, Nina has made a name for herself with thoughtful and quietly assertive dishes such as this one. Born in Italy and raised in New York City, she learned to cook while observing her mom and developed her skills under the watchful eye of Chef Nancy Silverton. Since the birth of her daughter, Indigo, Nina has become an even more fervent champion of farmers' markets and organic produce, which she uses to full effect in all her edible creations, including this one.

Makes 4 servings

1 pound albacore tuna, cut into 1-inch steaks, skin and bloodline removed

Kosher salt

2 Cara Cara or navel oranges

1 lemon

2 Fresno chiles or jalapeños

1 large fennel bulb

4 cups olive oil, plus more for the dressing

1 bunch fresh thyme sprigs

1 bunch fresh oregano sprigs

1 shallot, thinly sliced

4 garlic cloves, crushed

1 cup dry white wine

2 tablespoons pitted and halved Kalamata olives (halved lengthwise)

10 fresh basil leaves, gently torn

½ bunch fresh flat-leaf parsley, stems picked and leaves left whole

Freshly ground black pepper

1 tablespoon chopped fresh chives

4 slices toasted rustic bread, for serving (optional)

Place the tuna steaks on a baking sheet. Season both sides of each steak with salt and let them come to room temperature for 1 hour.

Meanwhile, zest the oranges and lemon and set aside the zest. Cut off the remaining white pith of the oranges in a curved slicing motion to reveal the fruit. Run a paring knife along each segment to release it from the membrane. Put the segments in a bowl and set aside.

Cut the lemon in half. Juice one half into a small bowl. Thinly slice the chiles, add them to the bowl of lemon juice, and set aside. Remove the top and core of the fennel bulb and thinly slice it with a mandoline or a sharp knife. Reserve some fennel fronds for garnish. Store the slices in ice water to keep them crisp.

In a large pot, combine the oil, orange zest, lemon zest, thyme, oregano, shallot, garlic, and white wine. Bring the oil to a simmer and heat until the temperature reaches 160°F. Place the tuna steaks in the oil and cover the pot. Let the steaks slowly poach for 15 minutes. Remove from the heat.

Remove the tuna from the oil. Using your hands, break the steaks into long bite-size pieces and place them in a bowl. (Don't use a fork, as it will look like shredded tuna from a can.) Once the poaching oil has cooled, cover the tuna, and let it rest while you prepare the salad.

In a separate large bowl, combine the orange segments, fennel slices, the chile-lemon juice mixture, olives, basil, and parsley. Toss with 1½ teaspoons olive oil, ¼ teaspoon salt, and the juice of the remaining lemon half. Taste and adjust the seasoning if necessary.

When the tuna is completely cooled, drain the oil. (The oil can be reused within a few days if thoroughly strained through a cheesecloth or a fine-mesh strainer.) Season the tuna with a pinch each of salt and pepper. To serve, spread a layer of tuna on each plate and top with a layer of salad, followed by a second layer of tuna, then a final layer of salad. Garnish with the chives and fennel fronds. Drizzle some olive oil around the perimeter of each plate. Accompany with slices of rustic bread that have been gently crisped in olive oil in a sauté pan over medium heat until golden.

FISH IN PARCHMENT
WITH HERB SAUCE

Kristy Mucci

Kristy, a food stylist and recipe tester, knows a successful dish engages all your senses, so her entrée incorporates taste, touch, sight, sound, and smell. It's fun and interactive to tear open the paper packets that are part of the presentation, but the real thrill is that the fish comes to the table cooked and seasoned perfectly. Baking fish in parchment, a technique called *en papillote,* is surprisingly uncomplicated and the trick for anyone who thinks preparing fish at home is too complicated or fussy (or stinky).

Makes 4 servings

1 cup soft green herbs, finely chopped (see Tip)
Kosher salt
¾ cup olive oil
4 (6- to 8-ounce) boneless fish fillets (such as flounder, salmon, sole, or arctic char)
Freshly ground black pepper
Zest and juice of 1 lemon
Pitted olives (optional)

Preheat the oven to 400°F.

Mix the herbs, ½ teaspoon salt, and the olive oil in a bowl and set aside so the flavors can develop.

Cut four 20-inch-long sheets of parchment paper and fold each in half. Unfold the first parchment sheet. Place a fish fillet about 1 inch to the right of the fold and season with salt and pepper. Sprinkle the fillet with 1 teaspoon of the lemon zest and 1½ teaspoons of the lemon juice. Top with 2 tablespoons of the herb sauce and some olives (if using).

Fold the parchment paper loosely over the fish and make ¼-inch folds around the edges to create a half-moon shape. Be sure to press and crimp the perimeter while folding to seal the packets well. Repeat with the remaining fish fillets.

Place the sealed packets on a baking sheet and bake for 10 to 15 minutes, depending on the thickness of the fish. The packets will be slightly browned and puffed up. To serve, place each packet on a plate and make sure each guest has a sharp knife to cut his or her packet open.

Tip: Kristy says any combination of fresh parsley, dill, fennel fronds, cilantro, chives, tarragon, chervil, marjoram, thyme, and basil works for this recipe. Use the leaves and thin, tender stems, discarding any thick stems.

SAN BEI JI
(TAIWANESE THREE-CUP CHICKEN)

Danielle Chang

This hearty, one-pot dish gets its name from the three ingredients—sesame oil, rice wine, and soy sauce—that infuse the chicken and cook down into a flavorful sauce. It's a staple throughout Taiwan and a traditional postpartum recipe, says Danielle, who ate lots of Three-Cup Chicken after giving birth to her daughters. As the busy founder of Lucky Rice, an events and multimedia company that celebrates Asian culture, Danielle now delights in making this quick dish for her girls on weeknights. She serves it alongside steamed rice and topped with lots of fragrant Thai basil.

Heat the oil in a large wok or clay pot over medium-high heat. Add the ginger and garlic and stir-fry for about 1 minute. Add the chicken and cook until brown on all sides, about 10 minutes.

Add the rice wine, soy sauce, and sugar and stir to combine. Reduce the heat to low and cook for 20 minutes more, or until the liquid has reduced and coats the chicken.

Stir in the basil and remove the pot from the heat. Serve with steamed white rice.

Makes 4 servings

¼ cup sesame oil
1 (1½-inch) piece fresh ginger, peeled and smashed
10 to 12 garlic cloves, smashed
2 pounds skin-on chicken wings, thighs, and drumsticks (see Tip)
¼ cup rice wine
¼ cup soy sauce
1 tablespoon sugar
1 large bunch fresh Thai basil leaves, torn
Steamed white rice, for serving

Tip: Danielle likes to make this dish with bone-in, skin-on chicken that's been chopped into 2-inch pieces. You can ask your butcher to prepare it this way for you.

LEMONGRASS & GINGER-BRINED CHICKEN

Jessica Koslow

The bold Asian flavors of lemongrass and ginger in this brine infuse the chicken breast, taking it from boring to brilliant. Jessica, the chef/owner of the cult L.A. café Sqirl, certainly has a knack for transforming basic ingredients. It's why fans and first-timers alike queue up—sometimes for as long as an hour—for her modern take on comfort food. Jessica suggests pairing this chicken with a grain salad or some arugula with shaved cheese, lemon zest, and hazelnuts. You do need to start this recipe 48 hours in advance, but it's worth it, as brining the chicken is key.

Makes 4 servings

- 2 boneless chicken breasts, about ½ pound each (see Tip)
- 2 stalks fresh lemongrass, peeled and coarsely chopped
- 3 tablespoons peeled and coarsely chopped fresh ginger
- 1 garlic clove, coarsely chopped
- ¼ cup kosher salt
- 2 tablespoons sugar
- 2 tablespoons canola oil

Place the chicken breasts side by side in a large nonreactive vessel or a glass baking dish. In a blender, combine the lemongrass, ginger, garlic, salt, sugar, and 1 cup water and blend until smooth. Add 3 cups water and stir to combine (don't blend again). Pour the brine over the chicken. Cover and refrigerate for 2 days.

Adjust the oven rack to the center position and preheat the oven to 450°F.

Remove the chicken from the liquid and pat dry with a paper towel.

Heat the oil in a large oven-safe pan over medium-high heat until hot but not smoking. Add the chicken and cook for 3 minutes, or until deep golden brown. Be careful of oil splatters. Flip the chicken with tongs and cook for 1 minute more. Transfer the pan to the oven and bake for 9 minutes or until the chicken is cooked through and registers 165°F on a thermometer. Let the chicken rest for 5 minutes before serving.

Tip: Jessica prefers skin-on boneless chicken breasts. If you can't find them, just ask your butcher. But skinless is okay in a pinch.

ADOBONG MANOK SA GATA
(FILIPINO VINEGAR CHICKEN)

Nicole Ponseca

"Adobo is like one of the best pop/soul songs that brings together all these loud ingredients without muting any of them," says Nicole, the former advertising executive and Filipino cuisine evangelist who owns Maharlika and Jeepney restaurants in Manhattan. "It's sour. It's salty. It's garlicky. It's great. I really can't think of another dish so deceptively simple with average ingredients and yet so big in flavor and power." Don't leave out her special ingredient, the chicken livers. "It's the 'dirty dust' that adds an additional depth to the sauce."

Makes 2 servings

Chicken
1¼ cups cane vinegar or distilled white vinegar
¾ cup low-sodium soy sauce
1 to 1½ pounds chicken wings (or chicken parts of your choice)
Freshly ground black pepper
⅓ cup chicken livers (optional)
1½ teaspoons coconut oil
6 garlic cloves, minced
1 teaspoon honey
1 whole banana pepper
2 bay leaves
1 tablespoon whole black peppercorns
½ cup coconut milk

Tomato Relish
1 diced tomato
½ cup fresh cilantro, minced
½ cup diced red onion
1 teaspoon Filipino fish sauce

Cooked jasmine rice, for serving

Make the chicken: Combine ¼ cup of the vinegar and ¼ cup of the soy sauce in a medium bowl, add the chicken, cover, and marinate in the refrigerator for 1 hour.

Remove the chicken from the marinade and pat dry. Season with pepper to taste. If using the chicken livers, wash and pat them dry, coarsely chop, and set aside.

Heat the coconut oil in a pan large enough to hold all the chicken wings, over medium-high heat. Add the chicken and sear for 5 minutes, or until slightly brown. Don't stir—you want lots of brown bits to form in the bottom of the pan. Remove the chicken from the pan and set aside.

Add the garlic and stir-fry in the pan for 1 minute, or until aromatic. Add the livers and stir-fry for 3 minutes. Add the remaining 1 cup vinegar and boil for 5 minutes, making sure to stand back as the fumes from the vinegar are powerful. Scrape the pan with a rubber spatula to incorporate any brown bits from the chicken. Add the remaining ½ cup soy sauce, the honey, whole banana pepper, bay leaves, and whole black peppercorns and stir to combine. Return the chicken to the pan, cover, and simmer on low heat for 20 minutes.

Uncover, flip each piece of chicken, and pour in the coconut milk. Cover again and simmer for 10 minutes more. Remove the lid and simmer for 5 to 7 minutes more. (The longer you reduce the liquid, the saltier and more tangy the chicken will become, so adjust the timing based on preference.)

Remove from the heat, remove the bay leaves, stir to coat the chicken with the sauce, and let rest for 10 minutes.

Make the relish: Combine the tomato, cilantro, red onion, and fish sauce in a bowl.

Serve the chicken with some jasmine rice and a side of the tomato relish. Or wait 24 hours. Nicole says the dish is even better the next day.

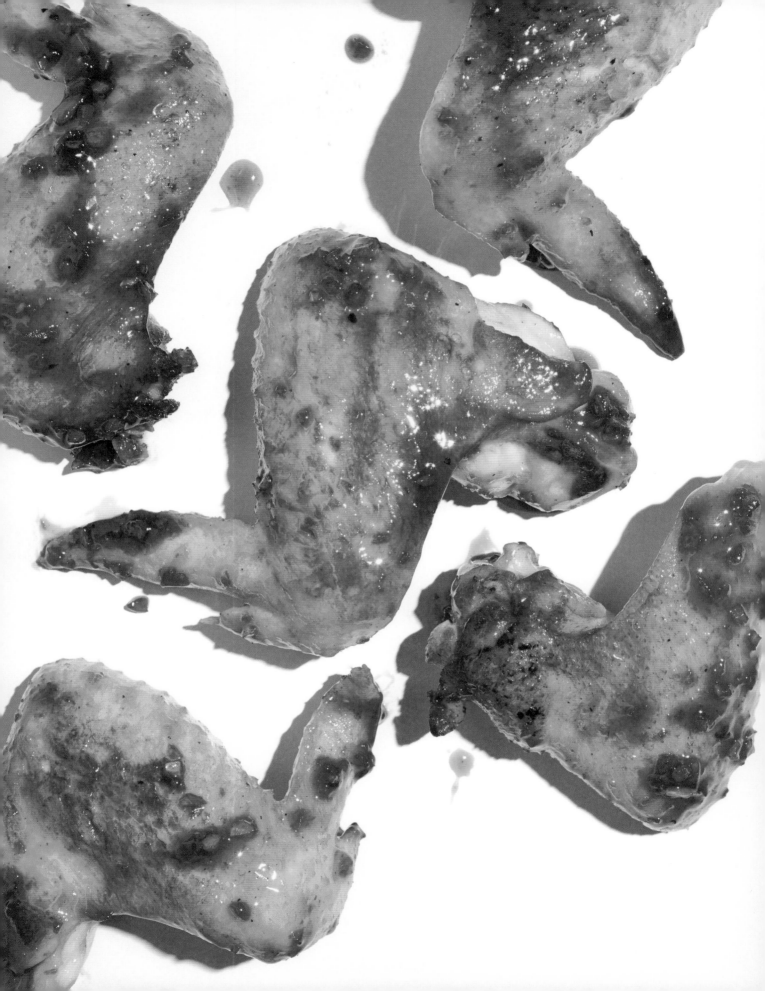

COCONUT CURRY
WITH CHICKEN & VEGETABLES

Danielle and Laura Kosann

This recipe should be in every busy gal's repertoire. Double it for extra guests, switch up the veggies based on what's in your fridge, add hotter peppers if you like things spicy, or make it vegan by eliminating the chicken. It's a weeknight go-to for the sisters behind *The New Potato*, the fashionable website that looks at life through the lens of food. "While we love recipes, we always encourage everyone to have fun with food," says Laura. "It's about the experience," adds Danielle. "Food doesn't always have to be so serious."

Heat 2 tablespoons of the coconut oil in a large saucepan over medium-high heat. Add the chicken and sauté until the chicken is lightly browned, then remove from the saucepan and set aside.

Heat the remaining 2 tablespoons coconut oil over medium heat. Add the garlic, ginger, and onion and sauté for 2 to 3 minutes, until the onion has softened.

Add the bell peppers, mushrooms, lemongrass, and bok choy and cook over medium-high heat until the vegetables have softened, about 5 minutes. Add the chicken and curry paste, stir, and cook for 2 minutes more.

Add the coconut milk, fish sauce, and jalapeño, then season with salt and pepper. Bring to a boil, then lower the heat to medium and simmer for 10 to 15 minutes, until the liquid has reduced slightly. Taste for seasoning and add more salt and pepper if necessary.

To serve, ladle the curry over jasmine rice, sprinkle with the cilantro, and garnish with lime wedges.

Makes 4 servings

4 tablespoons coconut oil
2 pounds boneless, skinless chicken thighs, cut into 1-inch pieces
3 garlic cloves, finely chopped
1 (1-inch) piece fresh ginger, peeled and finely chopped
½ yellow onion, chopped
3 red bell peppers, sliced
1 cup thinly sliced cremini mushrooms
2 stalks fresh lemongrass, peeled and finely chopped
1 large or 2 small heads bok choy, roughly chopped
1 tablespoon green curry paste
2 cups coconut milk
1 tablespoon fish sauce
1 tablespoon chopped jalapeño, seeded and membranes removed
Kosher salt and freshly ground black pepper
Cooked jasmine rice, for serving
½ cup chopped fresh cilantro, for serving
1 lime, cut into 4 wedges, for serving

MARAQ DIGAAG
(SOMALI CHICKEN STEW WITH YOGURT & COCONUT MILK)

Hawa Hassan

Rich with turmeric, cardamom, and ginger, this stew is a staple in Somali households and reflective of the rich flavors of East African cooking. Hawa, the CEO and "head saucier" at Basbaas Sauce, a line of Somali condiments, says that every woman in her family knows this recipe by heart and has passed it down to the next generation. Each puts her own spin on the stew; in the case of Hawa's mother, she adds red onion, which imparts an extra layer of sweetness. The *maraq digaag* is served with rice or greens—and a banana. Be sure to include the fruit. It's a Somali tradition.

Makes 8 servings

½ cup olive oil

2 red onions, chopped

2 large garlic cloves, minced

1 tablespoon minced fresh ginger

2 teaspoons kosher salt

1 tablespoon ground cumin

1 tablespoon curry powder

1 teaspoon turmeric powder

¼ teaspoon ground cardamom

5 tomatoes, roughly chopped

1 red bell pepper, seeded and membranes removed, roughly chopped

2 jalapeños, seeded and membranes removed if you want less heat, roughly chopped

1 cup plain yogurt

1 tablespoon tomato paste

1 potato, peeled and cubed

1 carrot, peeled and cut into coins

2 pounds boneless, skinless chicken thighs, cut into 1-inch pieces

1 (14-ounce) can coconut milk

1 cup chopped fresh cilantro

3 tablespoons ghee (optional)

Cooked jasmine rice, for serving

1 banana, peeled and sliced, for serving

Heat the olive oil in a large pot over medium heat. Add the onions and garlic and sauté for 5 minutes. Mix in the ginger, then stir in the salt, cumin, curry, turmeric, and cardamom.

In a blender or food processor, purée the tomatoes, bell pepper, and jalapeño, then add the mixture to the pot. Stir well. Add the yogurt and the tomato paste, cover, and cook for 10 minutes.

Add the potato and carrot, cover, and cook, stirring occasionally, for 30 minutes. Add the chicken, coconut milk, cilantro, and ghee (if using). Cover and cook until the sauce thickens slightly, about 20 minutes. Serve over rice with the sliced banana on the side.

BEER-BRINED ROAST CHICKEN

Adrienne Cheatham

Having worked at two very different New York hot spots—Red Rooster Harlem and Le Bernardin—Adrienne certainly knows about crave-worthy comfort food. But she credits her mom with the twist that makes this dish special—using beer as both the brine and the basting liquid. After the chicken absorbs the brine, it's rubbed with butter and set in a roasting pan surrounded by root vegetables and herbs. Before it's popped in the oven, beer is poured right into the pan. The end result? "The reduction makes a beautiful glaze and creates a deep, rich jus that is a delicious sauce for the chicken," says Adrienne.

Makes 4 servings

Chicken

1 cup kosher salt
⅔ cup packed light brown sugar
4 garlic cloves, lightly crushed
2 shallots, halved, with the root intact and outer skin removed
1 leek, white and light green parts only, quartered
7 sprigs fresh sage
5 sprigs fresh thyme
1 (4- to 4½-pound) chicken
3 (12-ounce) bottles lager

Vegetables

1½ pounds Brussels sprouts, ends trimmed, halved lengthwise
1½ pounds fingerling potatoes (or other small potato), halved lengthwise
2 cups whole peeled pearl onions
2 tablespoons chopped fresh sage, plus 4 sprigs
1 teaspoon lemon zest
2 tablespoons vegetable oil
¼ teaspoon kosher salt
Freshly ground black pepper

3 tablespoons unsalted butter, at room temperature
3 (12-ounce) bottles lager

Make the chicken: In a large pot, combine 8 cups water, the salt, and the sugar and bring to a simmer over medium-high heat, stirring to dissolve the salt and sugar. Remove from the heat and add the garlic, shallots, leek, sage, and thyme. Let cool to room temperature. Place the chicken breast-side down in a deep container. Pour the cooled brine over the chicken and add the beer until the chicken is submerged. Refrigerate overnight.

Preheat the oven to 350°F. Remove the chicken from the brine and pat dry inside and out with paper towels.

Make the vegetables: Combine the Brussels sprouts, potatoes, onions, chopped sage, and lemon zest in a bowl. Add the oil, salt, and pepper. Toss to coat everything evenly.

Place half the vegetables in the bottom of a roasting pan or large oven-safe sauté pan and put the chicken on top. Coat the top of the chicken breast and legs evenly with the butter. Pour 2 bottles of beer into the pan and arrange the sage sprigs around the chicken.

Roast the chicken and the vegetables, basting frequently with the liquid in the pan, for 30 minutes. Make sure the liquid doesn't completely evaporate from the pan. If it does at any point, add some of the extra beer.

Place the remaining vegetables on a rimmed baking sheet and place on a low rack. Roast the vegetables and the chicken for 20 to 30 minutes, occasionally stirring the vegetables and basting the chicken, until the chicken skin is brown and crisp and the vegetables are just tender and slightly charred.

Move the chicken to a platter and let it rest for 10 minutes before carving. If the liquid in the pan is thin, reduce it over medium-high heat. Serve the sliced chicken and roasted vegetables with a drizzle of the reduced cooking liquid on top.

CARNE ADOVADA
(MEXICAN SLOW-COOKED CHILE-BRAISED PORK)

Dominica Rice-Cisneros

This dish comes out of the oven melt-in-your-mouth perfect. Not only is it deeply flavorful, but for Dominica—the chef/owner of Oakland's Cosecha, the spot for tacos, tamales, and more—it brings back memories. The recipe is inspired by her grandmother Carmen, who migrated on horseback from Chihuahua, Mexico, to California at the age of eleven. Dominica spent time with Carmen in the kitchen sorting beans, preparing sauces, and learning other skills. "Her meals told the story about my family's journey and my own food history," she says. Dominica likes to serve the *carne adovada* with warm tortillas and homemade beans.

Makes 6 to 8 servings

3 pounds bone-in pork shoulder

2 tablespoons kosher salt

1 teaspoon cumin seeds, toasted and ground

1 teaspoon Mexican oregano, ground

1 large onion, diced

6 garlic cloves, sliced

1 (12-ounce) bottle Mexican beer

6 ounces dried guajillo chile or New Mexico chile, seeded

6 to 8 tortillas, warmed, for serving

Lime wedges, for serving

Sliced red onion, for serving

Fresh cilantro, for serving

Preheat the oven to 350°F.

Place the pork in a Dutch oven with a lid and season it with the salt, cumin, and oregano. Cover the pork with the onion and the garlic, pour the beer over everything, and set aside.

In a dry skillet, toast the chiles for 3 minutes. Place the chiles in a small pot with 2 cups water, bring to a simmer, and cook for 10 minutes. Transfer the chiles and their cooking liquid to a blender and purée until smooth. Strain the liquid through a fine-mesh strainer over the pork roast.

Cover the Dutch oven with the lid and bake for 2½ hours or until fork-tender. Let rest for 20 minutes, then transfer to a serving platter. Spoon the braising liquid on top and serve with tortillas, lime wedges, red onion, and cilantro.

VINDALOO BBQ BABY BACK RIBS

Preeti Mistry

These spicy grilled ribs exemplify Preeti's culinary style, which puts a contemporary and seasonal spin on Indian cuisine. "A little Indian, a little American, a lot of playfulness—and seriously damn good soulful food," says the chef/owner of Juhu Beach Club in Oakland. The ribs, with meat that falls off the bone, are a crowd-pleaser, and Preeti loves to make them for parties. They went over especially well when Preeti and her wife, Ann Nadeau, served them at their backyard wedding reception in 2014. The two opened Juhu Beach Club in 2013 in part to showcase Preeti's cooking—and to open guests' eyes and palates to what modern Indian food can be.

**Makes 20 to 26 ribs
(4 to 6 servings)**

4 cups white wine vinegar

2 cups fresh curry leaves

1 cup dried red chile de árbol (reduce the amount for a less spicy marinade)

1 tablespoon minced fresh ginger

1 tablespoon minced garlic

1 teaspoon cumin seeds

1 tablespoon kosher salt, plus more as needed

2 racks baby back ribs

½ cup tomato paste

½ cup packed light brown sugar

½ cup chopped fresh cilantro, for garnish

Coleslaw or creamy potato salad, for serving

Put the vinegar, curry leaves, chile, ginger, garlic, cumin, and salt in a blender and purée until smooth. Pour half the marinade over the ribs and refrigerate for at least 6 hours or overnight. Refrigerate the remaining marinade.

Preheat the oven to 300°F.

Remove the ribs from the sauce, wrap tightly in aluminum foil, and place on a baking sheet. Bake for 2 to 2½ hours, until the meat is done and the ribs have a bend to them when picked up. Let cool.

To make the BBQ sauce, put 2 cups of the remaining marinade in a small saucepan over medium heat. Add the tomato paste and brown sugar. Bring to a simmer, stirring frequently. When the sugar has dissolved and the ingredients are fully incorporated, taste and add more salt if necessary.

Heat a grill to medium-high. Cut the meat into individual or two-rib pieces. Place the ribs on the grill and baste with the sauce until well coated and warmed through. Serve with the remaining sauce on the side and garnish with the cilantro. Preeti likes to pair the ribs with coleslaw or creamy potato salad.

Tip: To make ahead, refrigerate the ribs after cooking in the oven and letting them cool. When ready to grill, make the BBQ sauce and cut and prepare the ribs as directed. "The ribs are actually easier to cut if you cook them a day in advance and chill them overnight," says Preeti.

BRISKET
WITH SWEET & SOUR ONIONS

Jessamyn Rodriguez

When someone tells you her brisket is her "crowning glory," you drop everything and you make that brisket. "Cook it low and slow and I promise you a brisket you can serve with pride," says Jessamyn. Brisket boasts aside, Jessamyn is best known for baked goods and for doing good. She's the founder and CEO of Hot Bread Kitchen, the New York–based social enterprise that helps immigrant women and others launch careers and food businesses. When you make Jessamyn's brisket, save some for sandwiches and make them with challah or brioche. (Just FYI, you can order those breads from Hot Bread's website for overnight delivery!)

Makes 10 servings

5 pounds brisket, fat layer intact (ask your butcher for a piece with at least ¼ inch of fat)
Kosher salt and freshly ground black pepper
4 yellow onions, sliced into thin rounds, plus more if needed
4 garlic cloves, minced
¼ cup ketchup
2 tablespoons tomato paste
1 tablespoon soy sauce
1 tablespoon dark brown sugar
¼ cup chopped fresh cilantro or parsley

Preheat the oven to 300°F and adjust the racks to accommodate a large, lidded roasting pan with a heavy bottom or a Dutch oven. The pan should be large enough for the meat to lie flat.

Generously season both sides of the brisket with salt and pepper and set aside.

Spread the onions over the bottom of the roasting pan or Dutch oven, adding extra onion slices as needed to completely cover the bottom.

In a bowl, combine the garlic, ketchup, tomato paste, soy sauce, brown sugar, ¼ teaspoon salt, and ¼ teaspoon pepper. Spread half the sauce on the non-fatty side of the brisket, massaging it into the meat. Place the brisket, sauce-side down, on top of the onions. Spread the remaining sauce on the fatty side of the brisket. Put the lid on the pan.

Bake for 3 to 4 hours, or until the meat shreds easily with a fork. Remove the lid and bake for about another hour, until the onion and the liquids have reduced to a thick sauce. Remove from the oven and let cool for 30 minutes.

Slice the brisket against the grain into ¼-inch-thick pieces.

To serve, lay the brisket slices on a serving platter. Using a spoon, remove and discard some of the fat floating on the onions at the bottom of the pan. Spoon the onion reduction over the brisket and top with the cilantro. Serve any leftover onion reduction in a gravy boat.

Tip: To serve the brisket later, lay the slices in another roasting pan, cover with aluminum foil, and refrigerate. Transfer the onion reduction from the pan to a large jar and refrigerate. The brisket and onions will keep for up to 5 days. When ready to serve, remove and discard the layer of fat from the top of the sauce. Spoon the rest of the sauce over the brisket and cover with foil. Warm for 30 minutes in a 300°F oven and serve according to the recipe. To make sandwiches, heat the slices in a skillet (Jessamyn prefers cast iron) over medium-high heat until they start to brown and the fat and edges get crispy, about 2 minutes on each side. Toast the bread or rolls you plan to use, spread with some warmed-up onion reduction, add the meat, sprinkle with cilantro, and enjoy.

SHROOMY CHEESEBURGERS
WITH MAPLE THYME CARAMELIZED ONIONS

Erin Fairbanks

A basic burger is so good and iconic we could be accused of gilding the lily here. But one bite of this and you won't care. The ground beef is mixed with chopped button mushrooms for a hint of earthy flavor, while Vidalia onions are deliciously caramelized thanks to maple syrup and balsamic vinegar. Erin, the former executive director of Heritage Radio Network, home to dozens of food podcasts, including Radio Cherry Bombe, says to buy the best ground beef you can afford from a source you trust. She's a big believer in helping transform the food system by supporting ethical producers and independent farmers.

Makes 4 burgers

Burgers

4 ounces button mushrooms, finely shredded
1 pound ground beef, 80/20 lean-to-fat ratio
Kosher salt

Caramelized Onions

4 tablespoons (½ stick) unsalted butter
2 large Vidalia onions, thinly sliced
3 tablespoons maple syrup
2 tablespoons balsamic vinegar
2 garlic cloves, minced
1 teaspoon kosher salt
Freshly ground black pepper
1 teaspoon lemon zest
1 tablespoon fresh thyme, finely chopped

Kosher salt and freshly ground black pepper
4 slices cheddar cheese
4 burger buns
3 tablespoons mayonnaise (optional)
1 tablespoon ketchup (optional)
4 butter lettuce leaves

Make the burgers: In a medium bowl, mix the mushrooms, beef, and a pinch of salt until well combined. Refrigerate the mixture for about 1 hour.

Meanwhile, make the caramelized onions: Melt the butter in a large skillet over medium-high heat. Add the onions to the pan, turn the heat to medium-low, and cook, stirring frequently, for 20 minutes, until the onions are soft and translucent but not browned.

Add the maple syrup, vinegar, garlic, salt, and some pepper to the pan. Cook for 20 to 30 minutes more, or until the onions are soft, brown, and caramelized. The slower you cook them and the lower the heat, the better. When done, turn off the heat and stir in the lemon zest and thyme. Taste and season with a pinch more salt if necessary.

Preheat the oven to 350°F.

Shape and cook the burgers: Remove the meat from the fridge and heat a cast-iron skillet over medium-high heat. Form the meat into 4 equal patties. Sprinkle the top and bottom of each with a pinch of salt and some black pepper.

Drop your burger patties into the hot ungreased pan. Cook for 3 minutes, rotate the burgers (don't flip them yet), and cook for 1 minute more. Once the burgers have a nice dark-brown crust, turn down the heat slightly, flip the burgers, and cook to your liking, 2 to 4 minutes more. Place a slice of cheese on top of each burger halfway through. Remove the burgers from the pan, set on a plate, and loosely cover with aluminum foil. Allow the burgers to rest for 3 to 4 minutes.

Split the buns, place them cut-side down on a baking sheet, and toast in the oven for 3 to 5 minutes. Meanwhile, in a small serving bowl, mix together the mayonnaise and ketchup (if using). Smear the mayonnaise mixture on one side of each bun, top with a lettuce leaf, then a burger, and finish with a big spoonful of onions.

PYTTIPANNA
(SWEDISH MEAT & POTATO HASH)

Emma Bengtsson

This Swedish comfort food, with crispy cubed potatoes, seared beef, and browned onions, is similar in concept to American hash. It's traditionally topped with a fried egg and served with a side of pickled beets and cucumbers. *Pytt*, as it's called in Sweden, came about as a way to use up leftovers, but Emma, a Nordic chef who grew up in a small town on the country's west coast, prefers top-notch ingredients, including high-quality meat. As the chef of Aquavit in Manhattan, Emma is celebrated for her elevated take on her country's cuisine, but she still loves simple dishes from back home.

Peel the potatoes and cut them into ½-inch cubes, dropping the cubes into a large bowl of cold water as you work so they don't oxidize. Drain the potatoes.

Melt 4 tablespoons of the butter in a large nonstick skillet or cast-iron pan over medium heat. Add the potatoes and cook for 10 to 12 minutes, until golden brown and crispy. Don't stir too frequently, or the potatoes will fall apart. Add the onion and cook for about 2 minutes, until translucent. Transfer the onions and potatoes to a plate.

Add 1 tablespoon of the butter to the skillet and stir in the beef cubes. Cook for 3 to 4 minutes, until the meat has a nice sear. Be careful not to overcook the meat. Season with salt and pepper, add the potatoes and onions, and stir to combine.

Melt the remaining 1 tablespoon butter in a large skillet over medium heat. Crack in the eggs one at a time. Cook until the whites have set, 3 to 4 minutes. Serve the hash with a fried egg on top of each portion and, if desired, a side of pickled beets and cucumbers.

Makes 4 servings

- 2 pounds waxy potatoes
- 6 tablespoons (¾ stick) unsalted butter
- 1 medium yellow onion, diced
- 8 ounces beef brisket, cut into ½-inch cubes
- 8 ounces beef strip steak, cut into ½-inch cubes
- Kosher salt
- Freshly ground black pepper
- 4 large eggs
- Pickled beets and cucumbers, for serving (optional)

BAKED EGGS
WITH LEEKS & DANDELION GREENS
Aran Goyoaga

The writer–photographer–food stylist behind the blog *Cannelle et Vanille* first cooked this dish for an impromptu brunch with friends at her Seattle studio. Rich with spring greens, it's a tribute to Aran's paternal grandparents and her childhood visits to their farm in the Basque Country. Her grandmother always made baked eggs, and leeks and other vegetables were plentiful, so much so that they would send her family home with bagsful. "I remember the smell of leeks in my dad's Seat 132 car for days and days after," she says.

Makes 4 to 6 servings

3 tablespoons olive oil
1 medium leek, sliced (see Tip)
1 small yellow onion, thinly sliced
2 garlic cloves, minced
½ teaspoon kosher salt, plus more as needed
Freshly ground black pepper
4 cups chopped dandelion greens (escarole also works well)
½ cup heavy cream
4 ounces goat cheese
6 large eggs
2 tablespoons finely chopped fresh chives
2 tablespoons finely chopped toasted almonds

Preheat the oven to 350°F.

Heat the olive oil in a medium oven-safe sauté pan or cast-iron skillet over medium-high heat. Add the leek, onion, and garlic, then sprinkle with the salt and season with pepper. Reduce the heat to medium and cook, stirring frequently, until the vegetables are soft and beginning to caramelize, about 7 minutes.

Add the dandelion greens and cook for 2 to 3 minutes more, until wilted. Remove the pan from the heat.

Pour the heavy cream over the vegetables and dot with pieces of the goat cheese. Crack the eggs one at a time and nestle them evenly on top of the vegetables. Sprinkle each yolk with a tiny pinch of salt and some pepper.

Bake the eggs until the whites are set but the yolks are still soft, about 10 minutes. Check frequently so as not to overcook the yolks.

Sprinkle with the chives and almonds, then slice and serve while warm.

Tip: When preparing the leeks, first cut off the dark green tops and ¼ inch from the bottoms, including the roots, then cut the leek in half lengthwise. Rinse carefully under cool running water to remove any sand or grit between the layers.

SAVORY OATMEAL
WITH MISO & MUSHROOMS

Lexie Smith

Lexie, a Brooklyn-based artist and baker, gives oatmeal the dinner treatment here. Miso makes this super savory and lends a hint of cheese flavor, while the egg adds creaminess. As the recipe is gluten-free, it's perfect for those with tummy issues. "When I was in my teens, I noticed that most of the things I was eating made me feel worse instead of better and I set out to understand why," says Lexie. Realizing she had control over what she ate and how she felt was liberating. Lexie says "follow your gut"—good advice for cooking, eating, and living.

Makes 4 servings

- 1 tablespoon olive oil, plus more as needed
- 2 heaping cups oyster mushrooms, torn into large pieces
- Kosher salt
- 1 spring onion or 2 scallions, sliced (whites and greens separated)
- 2 cups quick-cooking gluten-free oats
- 1 large garlic clove
- Freshly ground black pepper
- 1 large egg
- 4 teaspoons tamari
- 4 teaspoons white miso
- 1 teaspoon toasted sesame seeds
- ¼ teaspoon coarse sea salt
- Yogurt, for serving (optional)

Heat the olive oil in a heavy-bottomed pan over medium-high heat. Add the mushrooms and ¼ teaspoon salt and toss, drizzling with a bit more oil if necessary. Cover and cook for a few minutes, stirring once, until the mushrooms are soft and beginning to brown. Add the whites of the spring onion and cook for another minute or so, until the onion has softened slightly. Remove the pan from the heat and set aside.

Put the oats in a medium saucepan and add 3¼ cups water. Grate the garlic clove into the water using a fine grater or Microplane and add ¼ teaspoon salt and some pepper. Cook over medium-high heat, stirring gently and adjusting the amount of water as needed, until bubbles begin to form on the surface and most of the water has been absorbed, about 5 minutes.

Turn the heat to medium-low and crack the egg into the middle of the oatmeal. Stir quickly and continuously for a few minutes. The egg will cook and help thicken the oatmeal. Do not let the mixture bubble too rapidly or the egg might curdle. The oatmeal should be thick and stick to your spoon.

Whisk in the tamari and miso, making sure to break up any clumps. Add a tablespoon or more of water if you prefer a looser consistency.

Turn off the heat and mix in the spring onion greens. Divide the oatmeal among four bowls and top with the mushrooms, sesame seeds, sea salt, and a drizzle of olive oil. Add some yogurt, if desired.

Tip: Have some seasonal veggies you love? Throw them in. "Garlic scapes are really nice here, as is asparagus, leafy greens, or roasted winter squash," says Lexie.

SOUPS & SALADS

WATERMELON GAZPACHO

Melia Marden

Nothing highlights the beauty of summer produce like gazpacho. Melia, the chef behind Manhattan's The Smile and The Smile to Go, mixes things up with the addition of watermelon, a sweet complement to the traditional base of tomato and cucumber. On a sweltering night in July or August, why make anything else? Melia's love for gazpacho began on a trip to Spain, the summer after her college graduation. Upon her return, she set about making her ideal version, which you can sometimes find on the menu at her restaurants.

Makes 6 servings

6 medium tomatoes, coarsely
    chopped

4 cups chopped seedless watermelon

2 medium cucumbers, peeled and
    coarsely chopped

½ medium red onion, coarsely
    chopped

½ cup plus 2 tablespoons olive oil

3 tablespoons red wine vinegar

1½ teaspoons kosher salt,
    plus more as needed

8 fresh basil leaves, cut into
    thin strips

¼ teaspoon flaky sea salt

Combine the tomatoes, watermelon, cucumbers, onion, ½ cup of the olive oil, the vinegar, and the salt in a large bowl. Let sit for 10 minutes to allow the flavors to come together.

Working in batches, pour the ingredients into a blender or food processor and purée on high until completely smooth, about 2 minutes. Return the soup to the bowl and taste for seasoning. Add more salt if needed. Refrigerate the soup for 1 hour, until cold.

To serve, ladle the soup into chilled bowls and drizzle with the remaining 2 tablespoons olive oil. Sprinkle with the basil and the sea salt and serve.

SPRING GREENS BORSCHT

Victoria Granof

One of the most admired food stylists around, Victoria learned about this special soup while living in a small Ukrainian village waiting for her son's adoption to be approved. "There was nothing to do all day except read and visit the market, where there were a lot of skinny chickens and dairy products, but no green vegetables or anything grown aboveground," she remembers. "Finally, one day, there were elderly ladies in headscarves standing outside the market, clutching small bunches of ramps and sorrel. One of the nurses at the orphanage said I must make borscht with the greens and told me how." Now Victoria makes the soup every May in celebration of spring and her son's adoption.

Makes 4 servings

4 small boiling potatoes
Kosher salt
1 tablespoon sunflower oil or unflavored vegetable oil
2 tightly packed cups chopped spring alliums (such as spring onions, ramps, green garlic, scallions, and/or leeks), whites and greens separated
2 tightly packed cups spring greens (such as sorrel, wild fennel, dill, and/or spinach)
4 cups whey (see Tip)
2 cups chicken or vegetable broth
¼ teaspoon freshly ground white pepper, plus more as needed
¼ cup fresh lemon juice (optional)
2 large hard-boiled eggs, peeled and coarsely chopped
8 ounces Greek yogurt

Place the potatoes in a saucepan, add cold water to cover, and salt the water. Bring to a boil, then turn the heat down to medium and simmer for 15 to 20 minutes, or until the potatoes offer no resistance when pierced with a fork. Turn off the heat and keep the potatoes warm in the water.

Heat the oil over medium-high heat in a large saucepan. Add the white parts of the allium bulbs and sauté until they become translucent and begin to take on some color, 5 to 7 minutes. Add the allium greens and the spring greens and sauté for 5 minutes more. Stir in the whey and the broth. Add ¼ teaspoon salt and the pepper and bring to a boil. Turn the heat down to medium-low and simmer for 15 to 20 minutes.

Transfer the soup to a food processor or blender and purée until the soup is as smooth or as chunky as you prefer—be careful when blending hot liquid. Taste and add more salt and pepper if needed. If the soup isn't tangy enough, add the lemon juice.

Cut each potato into quarters. Ladle the soup into four bowls and divide the potatoes evenly among them. Garnish with the egg and a dollop of yogurt and serve.

Tip: You can find whey in specialty grocery stores. Otherwise, feel free to substitute broth.

CHICKEN MEATBALLS
IN ROASTED LEMON BROTH

Sarah Hymanson and Sara Kramer

Here's a technique we never knew about: roasting lemon halves until puffy and caramelized so they release a deeply aromatic, concentrated juice. It's the centerpiece of this soup and brightens the broth immensely, making it the perfect base for mini meatballs, veggies, and creamy potatoes. This recipe was inspired by a friend's grandmother's soup that Sarah and Sara tasted while in Israel. Their love of Middle Eastern flavors—so evident at their popular L.A. eateries, Madcapra and Kismet—are on full display here.

Makes 5 servings

Meatballs
½ cup pine nuts
1 leek, white and light green parts, only, finely diced
1 fennel bulb, finely diced
2 shallots, finely diced
3 sprigs fresh thyme
2 tablespoons olive oil
Kosher salt
1 pound ground chicken (dark meat only)
Freshly ground black pepper

Broth
2 lemons, halved
¼ cup olive oil
1 shallot, halved with the root intact and outer skin removed
3 bay leaves
½ cinnamon stick
8 cups unsalted chicken broth
1½ teaspoons crushed dried mint
Kosher salt
4 cups cubed potatoes (use fingerlings or another small creamy variety)
4 cipollini onions, halved and sliced into ¼-inch half-moons
1 bunch hearty spinach, long stems trimmed

Make the meatballs: Toast the pine nuts in a dry skillet over medium heat for about 5 minutes, tossing them several times so they cook evenly. Transfer to a plate and let cool. Once cool, coarsely chop the nuts.

Combine the leek, fennel, shallots, thyme, olive oil, and ½ teaspoon salt in a medium skillet. Sweat over medium-low heat until everything is soft, about 10 minutes. Remove the thyme and let the mixture cool.

In a large bowl, combine the cooked vegetables, pine nuts, chicken, 2 teaspoons salt, and several cracks of pepper. Cover and refrigerate.

Make the broth: Preheat the oven to 400°F.

Roast the lemon halves cut-side up on a baking sheet for at least 45 minutes, until the lemons are puffy and the bottom ends are browned. Let the lemons cool and deflate, then squeeze them over a strainer or sieve to catch any pulp and seeds. Set the juice aside. (You'll have about ¼ cup roasted lemon juice, depending on the size of your lemons.)

Heat the olive oil in a stockpot over medium heat. Place the shallot halves in the olive oil, cut-side down, and cook until well browned. Add the bay leaves and the cinnamon stick and swirl around a few times. Carefully add the broth, being mindful of the hot oil, and follow with the mint, a pinch of salt, and the potatoes. Slowly bring the broth to a light simmer, allowing the potatoes to absorb the flavors without breaking down.

After 20 minutes, or when the potatoes are just tender, remove the shallot and the cinnamon stick. Add the onions. Next, add the roasted lemon juice 1 tablespoon at a time. Taste the broth after each addition and adjust the seasoning.

Finish the meatballs: With lightly wet hands, form the chicken mixture into balls about 1 inch in diameter. (You should have 25 to 30 meatballs total.) When done, add the meatballs to the broth. Gently poach over medium heat for about 7 minutes, or until just cooked through. Right before removing from the heat and serving, add the spinach to the broth to wilt. Remove the bay leaves and serve.

ESCAROLE & CANNELLINI BEAN SOUP
WITH POLENTA SLICES

Laura Ferrara

This combination of beans and greens with buttery polenta slices is heart-warming and homey. Laura loves cooking recipes that reflect her Italian heritage and highlight the bounty of her farm, Westwind Orchard, in upstate New York. There they harvest a range of fruits and vegetables, raise bees, and tap maple trees. Laura is unique in the farming community in that by day she's a major fashion editor at *Glamour* magazine. Her working orchard is a family affair, where she, her husband, their son, and their moms all pitch in.

Roughly chop the escarole and rinse well in a colander.

In a large pot, sauté the garlic in the olive oil over medium-high heat until fragrant but not browned, stirring often, for about 2 minutes. Add the wet escarole and stir until all the greens wilt, about 2 to 3 minutes. Add 4 cups water and the salt, stir, and cover the pot. Cook for 5 minutes, then reduce the heat to low and cook, covered, for 5 minutes more.

Add the beans, some black pepper, and the red pepper flakes. Raise the heat to medium-low and cook, uncovered, for 5 minutes.

To serve, put a slice of polenta in the bottom of each bowl and ladle the soup on top. Drizzle with some olive oil and grate some Parmigiano-Reggiano over the soup.

Makes 4 to 6 servings

Soup

1 pound escarole
2 garlic cloves, thinly sliced
2 tablespoons olive oil, plus more for serving
2 teaspoons kosher salt
1 (15-ounce) can cannellini beans, drained but not rinsed
Freshly ground black pepper
¼ teaspoon crushed red pepper flakes
Polenta Slices (recipe follows), for serving
Parmigiano-Reggiano, for serving

POLENTA SLICES

In a medium pot, whisk together 5 cups cold water and the cornmeal. Set a timer for 45 minutes. Bring the mixture to a boil over medium-high heat, whisking a few times. Once the mixture starts sputtering, reduce the heat to low. Stir every few minutes. When 5 minutes remain on the timer, mix in the salt, pepper, and butter.

Grease a 9½-inch square pan (or a similarly sized rectangular pan) and pour in the polenta. (The pan size doesn't have to be exact, but the bigger the pan, the thinner the slices will be.) Let the polenta set at room temperature. After 30 minutes, cut the polenta into slices for serving. If you prefer, you can toast the polenta slices. Heat a pan over medium heat, brush the polenta slices with olive oil, and place in the pan. Cook for 5 minutes. Flip, cook the other side, then serve.

Leftover polenta will keep wrapped in plastic in the refrigerator for up to 4 days.

Makes 6 to 8 servings

1 cup medium or fine cornmeal (not instant)
1 teaspoon kosher salt, plus more as needed
Freshly ground black pepper
1 tablespoon unsalted butter, plus more for greasing the pan

LEMONY LENTIL STEW
WITH GINGER & TURMERIC

Andrea Gentl

This hearty but delicate stew is packed with good-for-you ingredients, including ginger, garlic, and Andrea's current obsession, turmeric. She developed the recipe while on a monthlong cleanse when she needed to cook food that her family would like, too. Food isn't the only family affair for Andrea: she and her husband are two of the most in-demand lifestyle photographers around, shooting under the moniker Gentl & Hyers. Their extensive travels influence what she cooks at home. "I always look to foreign lands for inspiration and new tastes," she says.

Makes 4 servings

2 tablespoons olive oil

2 garlic cloves, smashed and finely chopped

2 small shallots, finely chopped

1½ cups Petite Crimson lentils or toor dal (split pigeon peas)

¼ cup coconut oil

1 (1-inch) piece fresh ginger, peeled and finely chopped

1½ teaspoons fennel seeds

1 (1½-inch) piece fresh turmeric, peeled and finely chopped

1 preserved lemon, quartered and seeded

1 small dried Indian red chile

¼ teaspoon dried Aleppo pepper

½ teaspoon kosher salt, plus more as needed

Fresh cilantro and plain Greek yogurt, for serving (see Tip)

Warm the olive oil in a large heavy-bottomed pot or Dutch oven over medium heat. Add the garlic and shallots and sauté until translucent, 2 to 3 minutes. Don't let them brown.

Add the lentils, coconut oil, ginger, fennel seeds, and turmeric. Reduce the heat to low. Let the coconut oil melt into the spices and lentils for about 2 minutes to release the flavors and coat the lentils.

Tuck the lemon quarters into the lentils to melt down during the cooking process, then add the red chile, Aleppo pepper, salt, and 5 cups water. Cover the pot and simmer over medium heat for 40 minutes, or until soft and soupy. Stir occasionally to break up the preserved lemon and add more water if the mixture seems too dry. Remove the red chile before serving and taste for seasoning. Add more salt if necessary. Ladle into bowls and serve with a sprinkling of cilantro and a dollop of yogurt.

Tip: You can top this stew with whatever you're craving. Andrea's other suggestions include sprouted sunflower seeds, shaved baby radish, lentil sprouts, and black sea salt. She loves the stew over Chinese black rice or Forbidden rice.

SOUP JOU MOU
(HAITIAN PUMPKIN SOUP)

Leah Penniman

This recipe is tied directly to the mission of Soul Fire Farm, the organization cofounded by Leah and dedicated to ending racism and injustice in the food system. Steeped in tradition, Soup Jou Mou is served on New Year's Day to commemorate the 1804 slave uprising that resulted in Haiti's liberation from France. Leah, who is of Haitian descent, says the dish had been reserved for white enslavers and forbidden to those enslaved. Today, she makes the creamy vegan soup to honor her heritage and showcase the vegetables and herbs harvested from her land in upstate New York.

Makes 6 to 8 servings

1½ pounds Caribbean pumpkin (calabaza) or butternut squash, peeled, seeded, and cut into 1-inch chunks

3 tablespoons olive oil

1 tablespoon kosher salt, plus more as needed

1 celery stalk, chopped

1 large onion, chopped

½ pound green cabbage, chopped

2 leeks, white and light green parts only, chopped

2 potatoes (about ½ pound), chopped

2 carrots, chopped

1 turnip, diced

1 (14-ounce) can coconut milk

1 cup fresh or canned sweet corn

1 tablespoon chopped fresh flat-leaf parsley

1 whole Scotch bonnet pepper (or other spicy pepper)

4 garlic cloves, minced

½ teaspoon fresh thyme leaves

2 whole cloves

1 tablespoon fresh lime juice

¼ pound dried spaghettini (optional)

Freshly ground black pepper

Preheat the oven to 400°F.

In a large bowl, toss the pumpkin with 1 tablespoon of the olive oil and ¼ table-spoon salt. Transfer the pumpkin to a large baking sheet or roasting pan. Next, toss the celery, onion, cabbage, and leeks with 1 tablespoon of the olive oil and ¼ tablespoon salt. Transfer to a baking sheet or roasting pan. Last, toss the potatoes, carrots, and turnip with the remaining 1 tablespoon olive oil and ¼ table-spoon of the salt. Transfer to a baking sheet or roasting pan.

Place the pumpkin on the higher rack in the oven and the pans with the vegetables on the middle or lower rack and roast for 10 minutes. Remove each pan, toss gently, and return to the oven. (The cooking times on all three pans vary, so check for doneness. The celery-onion-cabbage-leek mixture will cook the fastest.) When everything is cooked through and tender, remove from the oven and let cool.

Transfer the cooled pumpkin to a blender or food processor, add the coconut milk, and puree. Transfer the mixture to a large pot and add 8 cups of water. Stir and bring to a low boil over medium-high heat. Stir in the roasted vegetables, corn, parsley, and whole hot pepper. Add the garlic, thyme, cloves, and lime juice and stir again. Reduce the heat to maintain a simmer and cook for 15 to 20 minutes to bring the flavors together. If you are using pasta, add it 10 minutes before the soup is done.

Before serving, remove the hot pepper. Stir in the remaining salt and season with black pepper. Taste and adjust the seasoning if necessary.

MIYEOKGUK
(KOREAN SEAWEED SOUP)

Sohui Kim

"It's a humble soup that has meaning and significance in my culture," says Sohui about this restorative brew, the recipe for which has been handed down by generations of women in her family. In fact, her mother made sure that Sohui ate *miyeokguk* every day for a month after giving birth to her first child. Her grandmother cooked it for her on birthdays and now Sohui, the chef behind The Good Fork and Insa restaurants in Brooklyn, makes it for her children.

Makes 10 servings

1 ounce dried wakame seaweed

2 tablespoons olive oil

1 pound beef chuck,
    cut into ½-inch cubes

10 garlic cloves, minced
    (about ⅓ cup)

2 tablespoons sesame oil

1 teaspoon mirin

1 teaspoon fish sauce, plus more
    as needed

2 teaspoons soy sauce, plus more
    as needed

1 teaspoon sea salt, plus more
    as needed

Freshly ground black pepper

3 scallions, white and light green
    parts only, thinly sliced, for serving

1 tablespoon sesame seeds, for
    serving

Soak the seaweed in 2 cups warm water for 5 to 10 minutes. Drain and chop into bite-size pieces.

Heat the olive oil in a large, heavy-bottomed pot over medium-high heat. Add the beef and sear for 5 to 7 minutes, until a nice brown crust develops. (Something known as a *fond*, or a browned base, should form on the bottom of the pan.) Add the garlic and sauté for 1½ minutes, until fragrant.

Add the seaweed and sesame oil and sauté for about 3 minutes, then add 12 cups water, the mirin, fish sauce, soy sauce, salt, and some pepper. Bring to a boil, then reduce the heat to low and simmer for about 1½ hours, until the meat is tender. Taste the broth and adjust the seasoning with more fish sauce, soy sauce, or salt.

To serve, garnish with the scallions and sesame seeds.

UME OCHAZUKE
(JAPANESE GREEN TEA WITH RICE & PICKLED PLUMS)

Sue S. Chan

Consider this the elegant answer to instant soup. Pour your favorite green tea over rice, embellish with savory garnishes, and you have a meal that's light and flavorful. "Homestyle Japanese dishes are really underappreciated in the States," says Sue, who loves this for breakfast. "They are hearty, yet healthy, and great for everyday eating." It's the perfect fuel for Sue, who was the brand director for Momofuku for almost seven years. She also cofounded Toklas Society, a professional empowerment group for women in the food and hospitality industries, and now runs her own communications and production agency called Care of Chan.

Makes 2 servings

1 cup Japanese short-grain rice

2 green tea bags, or 2 tablespoons loose green tea

½ teaspoon instant dashi powder

2 Japanese pickled plums (ume), pitted

¼ teaspoon toasted sesame seeds

1 sheet nori, cut into thin strips

2 shiso leaves, cut into thin strips

Salmon roe (optional)

Pickled ramps (optional)

1 teaspoon grated fresh or prepared wasabi

1 teaspoon grated fresh ginger

Rinse the rice under cold running water in a fine-mesh sieve until the water runs clear. Put the rice and 2 cups water in a medium saucepan and bring to a boil over medium-high heat. Reduce the heat to low, cover, and cook for 15 to 20 minutes, or until the rice is tender and all the water has been absorbed. Remove the rice from the heat and allow to rest for 10 minutes. Divide the rice between two bowls.

Boil 3 cups water in a saucepan. Add the green tea and steep according to the package directions. Discard the tea bags (or strain the tea to remove the loose tea leaves), then stir in the dashi powder until it has completely dissolved. Divide the green tea–dashi broth between the rice bowls.

Divide the plums, sesame seeds, nori strips, shiso, roe (if using), and ramps (if using) between the bowls, placing everything on top of the rice. Place half the wasabi and half the ginger on the rim of each bowl or in a small side dish. Mix in the wasabi and ginger a bit at a time as you enjoy the soup.

BLACK SESAME OTSU
WITH SOBA NOODLES & TOFU

Heidi Swanson

This unique soba noodle salad is refreshing and distinctly Heidi. The writer-photographer-globetrotter-shopkeeper has a knack for creating meditative meals that touch on her travels and delight the taste buds in the subtlest way. Her inspiration here was a dish she discovered at a tiny restaurant in San Francisco, her home base. The umami-packed black sesame paste that flavors this salad can be made a few days in advance and also tastes great on spinach, roasted potatoes, broccoli, and other veggies.

Makes 4 servings

1 teaspoon pine nuts

1 teaspoon hulled sunflower seeds

½ cup black sesame seeds

1½ tablespoons organic cane sugar

1½ tablespoons shoyu, tamari, or soy sauce

1½ teaspoons mirin

1 tablespoon toasted sesame oil

2 tablespoons brown rice vinegar

⅛ teaspoon cayenne pepper

Fine sea salt

12 ounces soba noodles

12 ounces extra-firm tofu

Olive oil

1 bunch scallions, white and light green parts only, thinly sliced

Toast the pine nuts and sunflower seeds in a large skillet over medium heat, shaking the pan regularly, until golden, about 3 minutes. Add the sesame seeds to the pan and toast for a minute or so. Remove from the heat as soon as you smell a hint of toasted sesame.

Transfer the nuts and seeds to a mortar and crush with a pestle; the texture should be like black sand. (Alternatively, you can use a mini food processor.) Stir in the sugar, shoyu, mirin, sesame oil, vinegar, and cayenne. Taste and adjust the seasoning if needed. Set aside.

Bring a large pot of water to a boil. Salt the water generously, add the soba, and cook according to the package instructions until tender. When done, reserve some of the cooking water and drain the noodles. Rinse the noodles under cold running water.

While the noodles are cooking, drain the tofu, pat dry with a paper towel, and cut into matchstick-size slivers. Season the tofu with a pinch of salt and toss with a small amount of olive oil. Cook the tofu in a large skillet over medium-high heat, tossing every few minutes, until browned on all sides.

Reserve a heaping tablespoon of the sesame paste, then thin the rest with ⅓ cup of the reserved noodle cooking water.

In a large bowl, toss the soba, half the scallions, and the sesame paste until well combined. Add the tofu and gently toss again. Serve topped with a dollop of the reserved sesame paste and the remaining scallions.

RED CABBAGE SALAD
WITH SESAME ANCHOVY VINAIGRETTE

Angela Dimayuga

This colorful salad packs crunch and depth of flavor into every bite. Cooling and complex, it's a nice counterpart to the fiery Sichuan dishes Angela cooks at Manhattan's Mission Chinese Food as executive chef. In fact, it's the first recipe she ever wrote for the restaurant when she started there in 2012. Angela has since made a name for herself with creations that are fusion by nature. In this case, she borrows from Jewish, Middle Eastern, and Japanese cuisines with the inclusion of kasha, tahini, and dried seaweed.

Heat the canola oil in a small saucepan over medium-high heat until it shimmers. Add the kasha and cook until the kernels have browned. Keep an eye on them, as they can quickly burn. Transfer to a paper towel–lined plate to cool and season with a pinch of salt.

In a small bowl, whisk together the lemon juice, vinegar, miso, tahini, soy sauce, and anchovies. If too thick, loosen the dressing with a bit of water. In a large bowl, toss the cabbage with the dressing until fully coated. Taste and season with more lemon juice and/or salt if needed.

On a flat serving plate, arrange the dressed cabbage, then place the beets on top. Sprinkle the fried kasha, sesame seeds, and aonori over the cabbage so that each bite has some of the garnish.

Makes 4 to 6 servings

- ½ cup canola oil
- 2 teaspoons kasha (roasted buckwheat kernels)
- Kosher salt, plus more if needed
- Juice of 1 lemon
- 1 tablespoon rice vinegar
- 2 tablespoons white miso
- 3 tablespoons tahini
- 1 tablespoon soy sauce
- 6 anchovy fillets, minced
- ½ head red cabbage, cored and cut into 1-inch pieces
- 1 baby beet, yellow or candy striped, peeled and sliced into ⅛-inch-thick disks
- 1 teaspoon toasted white sesame seeds
- 2 tablespoons aonori seaweed

CAESAR BRUSSELS SALAD

Julia Sherman

Julia, the creative force behind *Salad for President*, a website that celebrates both artists and leafy greens, combines sprouts with a retro dressing for a dish that's party perfect: It can be prepared ahead, it doesn't wilt or get soggy, and it makes for killer leftovers. Plus, it turns something virtuous into an indulgence, thanks to the creamy dressing. The recipe originated with Julia's mother, an early proponent of not cooking Brussels sprouts to death. The first time her mom shredded Brussels sprouts and served them raw, Julia thought she was a genius.

Makes 10 servings

Dressing

2 large egg yolks
2 tablespoons fresh lemon juice
5 oil-packed anchovy fillets, drained
3 tablespoons chopped fresh flat-leaf parsley, plus more for garnish
2 tablespoons chopped fresh chives
1 teaspoon Dijon mustard
1 teaspoon white wine vinegar
¼ cup olive oil
¼ cup grapeseed oil

Brussels Sprouts

2 pounds Brussels sprouts
¼ cup olive oil
3 tablespoons white wine vinegar
1½ teaspoons kosher salt
Freshly ground black pepper
1 garlic clove (optional)
½ cup freshly grated Parmigiano-Reggiano or Pecorino Romano cheese

Make the dressing: In a food processor, combine the egg yolks, lemon juice, anchovies, parsley, chives, mustard, and vinegar and process until the herbs are broken down into small green flecks. With the motor running, add the olive oil in a slow stream to emulsify, then add the grapeseed oil. Spoon the dressing into a squeeze bottle or container with a spout and refrigerate until ready to serve.

Make the Brussels sprouts: Wash and thoroughly dry the sprouts, removing any brown or damaged outer leaves. Trim the bottom of each sprout. If nice green outer leaves fall off, set them aside in a large salad bowl.

Gather 2 cups of the smallest sprouts and thinly slice them lengthwise. Add them, along with the fallen leaves, to the salad bowl.

In the food processor with the shredding disk attached, shred the remaining sprouts, then add them to the salad bowl. Dress with the olive oil, vinegar, salt, and pepper to taste. Grate the garlic (if using) into the mixture using a Microplane. Toss to combine. Set the Brussels sprouts aside to marinate for 30 minutes or up to 2 hours.

When ready to serve, squeeze or drizzle the dressing over the sprouts. Sprinkle the cheese generously over the top, garnish with parsley, and serve family-style.

PURPLE GRAIN ROASTED BEET & BARLEY SALAD

Martha Hoover

Barley goes from beige to brilliant thanks to a beet purée that coats every grain in this magenta-hued salad. The cranberries and grapes add tang and sweetness, while the pecans provide crunch. It's a versatile dish that works as a healthy vegetarian lunch or as a perfect accompaniment to turkey or pork. The recipe was created by Martha, the Indianapolis-based restaurateur and philanthropist, and it's a perfect example of the farm-to-table food she has championed for years. Today, Martha has a mini empire that includes her latest spot, Public Greens, which takes her beliefs one step forward: all profits go toward feeding hungry children.

Makes 8 servings

3 medium red beets

1½ cups barley

½ teaspoon kosher salt, plus more as needed

Freshly ground black pepper

½ teaspoon granulated sugar

½ cup toasted pecans, roughly chopped

2 tablespoons chopped fresh tarragon

1 cup dried cranberries

1 cup halved red grapes

1 cup balsamic vinegar

Preheat the oven to 400°F.

Wrap the beets in aluminum foil, place them on a baking sheet, and roast for 50 minutes, being sure to check them once or twice. The beets are ready when a knife slides into them easily. Remove from the oven, open the foil packet, and let cool. Peel and chop the beets and set aside.

Prepare the barley according to the package directions. You should end up with about 4 cups barley.

Place 1 cup of the beets, ¼ cup water, the salt, some pepper, and the sugar in a blender and purée. Transfer the beet purée and the barley to a large bowl and combine thoroughly.

Reserve some pecans and tarragon for garnishing. Mix in the remaining beets, cranberries, grapes, pecans, and tarragon. Taste for seasoning and add more salt and pepper if necessary.

Heat a pan over medium-high heat and add the vinegar, being mindful of any fumes. When the vinegar starts boiling, reduce the heat to medium-low and simmer until the vinegar has reduced by more than half and has a thick, syrupy consistency. Remove from the heat.

To serve, divide the salad among eight bowls. Drizzle each with the balsamic reduction and top with a sprinkle of tarragon and pecans.

"MILLION INGREDIENT" AUTUMN SALAD

Naomi Starkman

Not to objectify our fruit and veggies, but this is one good-looking salad. It's loaded with some of autumn's most eye-catching produce, including delicata squash, pomegranates, persimmons, and radicchio. Add crunchy walnuts, white balsamic vinaigrette, and Manchego cheese and you are set with a dreamy lunch or light dinner. An organic gardener and the editor in chief of *Civil Eats*, a daily website about the American food system, Naomi loves composing seasonal salads built around color, texture, and flavor. They're a tribute to the bounty of her backyard and all the farmers' markets she—and the rest of us—love so much.

Makes 6 servings

1 delicata squash, halved, seeded, and cut into ½-inch-thick half-moons

2 tablespoons plus ¼ cup olive oil

Kosher salt and freshly ground black pepper

2 tablespoons white balsamic vinegar

1 small head frisée (about ½ pound)

2 medium endives (about 10 ounces each), halved and cut into ½-inch pieces

1 small head radicchio (about 6 ounces), cored and torn into bite-size pieces

2 Fuyu persimmons, cored and thinly sliced

Seeds from 1 large pomegranate

½ cup chopped walnuts

¼ cup shaved Manchego cheese

Preheat the oven to 400°F.

Place the squash on a baking sheet and toss with the 2 tablespoons olive oil and ¼ teaspoon salt.

Roast for 10 minutes. Flip each squash piece, rotate the pan, and roast for 10 minutes more, or until golden brown. Remove from the oven and set aside to cool.

In a small bowl, whisk together the remaining ¼ cup olive oil, the vinegar, ¼ teaspoon salt, and pepper to taste.

On a large serving platter, place half the frisée, endive, and radicchio. Layer on half the persimmons, pomegranate seeds, and squash. Repeat with the remaining ingredients and drizzle the dressing on top. Toss lightly, sprinkle with the walnuts and shaved Manchego, and serve immediately.

SALMON SALAD
WITH FENNEL & NEW POTATOES
Melissa Clark

At *Cherry Bombe* HQ, we call Melissa the "Queen of Cookbooks." A *New York Times* columnist, she's coauthored dozens of books with some of the biggest names in the world of food and still delights in creating and testing recipes. Here, in this salad she developed, fennel plays a major role, as the licorice-flavored bulbs are sliced thin and mixed throughout and the fronds are blended into a green pesto that gets tossed with the tiny potatoes and slathered on the salmon fillets. As most people just chop off the fennel fronds and throw them away, it's a great way to rescue an ingredient from the compost pile.

Makes 6 servings

2 small fennel bulbs with fronds, halved lengthwise
½ cup fresh basil leaves, sliced
4 garlic cloves, finely chopped
6 anchovies, chopped
Zest and juice of 2 large lemons
½ teaspoon fine sea salt, plus more as needed
¾ cup plus 1 tablespoon olive oil, plus more for drizzling
½ cup plain Greek yogurt
3 tablespoons Dijon mustard
2 tablespoons thinly sliced shallot
1½ pounds tiny new potatoes
½ cup fresh or frozen English peas
4 (6-ounce) skin-on center-cut wild salmon fillets, pin bones removed
Freshly ground black pepper
Lemon wedges, for garnish

Cut off the tops of the fennel and separate the stalks from the fronds. Discard the stalks and coarsely chop the fronds. Measure out ¾ cup of fronds and place in a blender. Save the remaining fronds for garnish. Add the basil, garlic, anchovies, lemon zest, 1½ teaspoons of the lemon juice, and the salt. With the motor running, drizzle in ¾ cup of the olive oil and blend until smooth. Taste and add more salt if needed.

Spoon ¼ cup of the fennel frond purée into a small bowl and scrape the rest into a large bowl. Stir the yogurt into the purée in the large bowl. Don't worry if it appears slightly curdled, as it will emulsify when tossed with the potatoes. Stir the mustard into the purée in the smaller bowl.

Using a mandoline or sharp knife, cut the fennel bulbs into thin slices, the thinner, the better. Toss with the shallot slices, 1½ teaspoons of the lemon juice, a large pinch of salt, and the remaining 1 tablespoon olive oil. Let stand at room temperature until ready to use.

In a pot of generously salted water, boil the potatoes until just tender when pierced with a knife, about 15 minutes. Add the peas for the last 2 minutes of cooking (or for the last 3 minutes if frozen). Drain and halve the potatoes when cool enough to handle. Toss the warm potatoes and peas with the yogurt–fennel frond dressing.

While the potatoes cook, preheat the oven to 450°F. Line a baking sheet with aluminum foil.

Season the salmon with salt and pepper and place on the prepared baking sheet skin-side down. Slather the mustard–fennel frond mixture over the tops of the fillets. Bake until the fish is just cooked through, 8 to 10 minutes. Let cool for 10 minutes before serving. You want to serve the fish warm, not hot.

Scatter the peas and the potatoes on a large platter, leaving room in between. Lift large chunks of salmon up from the pan, leaving the salmon skin stuck to the foil. Arrange amid the potatoes and decorate with the marinated fennel slices. Drizzle with olive oil and lemon juice and sprinkle with salt and pepper. Scatter the reserved fronds over the top and serve with some lemon wedges.

HANGER STEAK & TOMATO SALAD
WITH SICHUAN VINAIGRETTE

Naomi Pomeroy

This steak salad shows off Naomi's abilities and inspirations. The chef/owner of Beast, a multi-course prix-fixe restaurant in Portland, Oregon, Naomi has made a name for herself as an uncompromising force in the kitchen. She considers mastering the perfect sear an essential culinary building block, so it's a natural choice for her to feature beautifully prepared hanger steak, a once-overlooked cut now beloved by chefs and butchers alike. The salad is a nod to the Asian culinary influences in the Pacific Northwest, represented on the menu at Expatriate, the cocktail bar Naomi shares with her husband, Kyle, just across the street from Beast.

Makes 4 servings

Vinaigrette

2 teaspoons Thai chili sauce
2 teaspoons black bean garlic sauce
1 teaspoon minced fresh ginger
1 teaspoon fish sauce
2 teaspoons rice wine vinegar
1 teaspoon soy sauce
2 teaspoons agave
1 tablespoon canola oil
1 tablespoon fresh lime juice

Steak & Salad

1 pound hanger steak, cut in half
1 teaspoon sea salt
Freshly ground black pepper
1 cup short-grain rice
2 cups coarsely diced seeded tomatoes
1 cup halved cherry tomatoes
1 tablespoon olive oil
2 tablespoons coarsely chopped fresh Thai basil
2 tablespoons coarsely chopped fresh mint
2 tablespoons coarsely chopped fresh cilantro
2 scallions, green parts only, thinly sliced on an angle
¼ cup peanuts
1 cup Fried Shallots (recipe follows; optional)
1 tablespoon Toasted Rice Powder (recipe follows; optional)

Make the vinaigrette: Combine the chili sauce, black bean garlic sauce, ginger, fish sauce, vinegar, soy sauce, agave, canola oil, and lime juice in a jar with a tight-fitting lid. Shake well.

Make the steak and salad: Preheat the oven to 400°F.

Season the steaks with the salt and pepper and bring to room temperature. Soak the rice for 30 minutes, rinse, then cook according to the package instructions. Toss all the tomatoes with the vinaigrette and set aside to macerate for at least 30 minutes.

Meanwhile, heat the olive oil in a hot cast-iron pan over very high heat. Add the meat and sear for 1½ minutes on each side, weighing down the meat with a plate while searing.

Remove the plate and place the pan with the steaks in the oven for 3 to 4 minutes. The steaks should feel firm on the edges, but still quite soft in the center, registering about 118 to 120°F on a thermometer inserted into the thickest part. Remove from the oven and cover the steaks loosely with aluminum foil. Let rest for 10 to 15 minutes, then slice the steaks across the grain on a strong angle. Set aside and allow the juices to collect.

Divide the rice among four plates or shallow bowls. Top with some tomatoes and dressing, followed by a few slices of steak and the juices, herbs, scallions, and peanuts. Finish each salad with a topping of shallots and toasted rice powder, if desired.

(recipe continues)

FRIED SHALLOTS

Makes about 1½ cups

4 large shallots
3 cups canola oil
½ teaspoon kosher salt

Peel the shallots and leave the stem end intact. Slice the shallots crosswise so the rings of the shallots are as thick as a nickel. Split them into three equal-size batches.

Heat the canola oil in a medium pot over high heat to 275°F. Line a baking sheet with paper towels or brown paper. Reduce the heat to medium-high. Add one batch of shallots to the oil and stir frequently with a slotted spoon to ensure even cooking. Cook for 2 to 4 minutes, until they're golden brown with a little bit of the white showing. They burn easily, so keep an eye on the pot.

Using a slotted spoon or wire skimmer, immediately remove the shallots from the oil. Spread them across the paper towels to help absorb any excess oil. Repeat with the remaining batches. Replace the paper towels when they become saturated.

Season the shallots with the salt and allow them to cool completely. The shallots can be stored in an airtight container lined with paper towels for up to 1 week.

TOASTED RICE POWDER

Makes ½ cup

½ cup Thai sweet rice

This is a popular ingredient in Thai cuisine. You can make your own, or buy some from an Asian specialty grocery or online.

Toast the rice in a dry pan over low heat, stirring frequently, for about 10 minutes. Remove the pan from the heat when the rice is the color of wheat and has a light, nutty, toasted taste.

Grind the rice in small batches in a clean coffee grinder until it resembles coarse grains of sand. Avoid grinding to a fine powdery texture. Store in a tightly sealed container for up to 5 days.

SIDES

ROASTED ASPARAGUS & SCALLIONS
WITH BURRATA

Kate Brashares

Roasted veggies get the royal treatment in this salad, as they're topped with creamy burrata, crunchy almonds, tangy green salsa, and zippy lemon zest. It's farm to table at its best, from the executive director of Edible Schoolyard NYC, an offshoot of the organization created by Alice Waters to help children eat better and understand where their food comes from. A big proponent of seasonal eating, Kate switches up the vegetables and the herbs based on what's available. During asparagus season, she always serves the salad with some chilled rosé and grilled bread.

Makes 4 to 6 servings

2 bunches scallions, ends trimmed and outer layer removed
1 bunch asparagus, woody ends trimmed
¼ cup olive oil
Kosher salt and freshly ground black pepper
1 small garlic clove, finely chopped
1 tablespoon capers, drained (don't use the salt-packed ones)
¾ cup fresh flat-leaf parsley
¾ cup fresh basil leaves
2 tablespoons red wine vinegar
2 tablespoons slivered almonds
1 (8-ounce) ball burrata
Zest of ½ lemon
¼ teaspoon flaky sea salt

Preheat the oven to 425°F.

Toss the scallions and asparagus with 1 tablespoon of the olive oil, ¼ teaspoon salt, and some pepper on a baking sheet. Roast for about 12 minutes, or until the vegetables are tender and slightly shriveled (see Tip). Remove from the oven and arrange the asparagus and scallions on a serving platter.

While the vegetables are roasting, place the garlic, capers, parsley, and basil on a cutting board and chop everything together into fine pieces. Transfer to a bowl, add the remaining 3 tablespoons olive oil and the vinegar, and stir to combine. The salsa should be very thick. Taste for seasoning and add salt if necessary.

Toast the almonds in a dry cast-iron or nonstick pan over medium heat for 3 to 4 minutes, until fragrant and golden brown, turning them frequently as they burn easily. Remove from the pan and transfer to a bowl.

Using your hands, tear the burrata into chunks over the serving platter (to catch any of the cream that's inside the cheese) and place over the roasted veggies. Spoon the salsa verde over the veggies and burrata, and sprinkle the almonds on top. Finish with the lemon zest and sea salt and serve.

Tip: The asparagus and scallions generally take the same time to roast. If you use one baking sheet, cook the scallions on one side and the asparagus on the other so you can easily remove whichever cooks faster.

PIPÉRADE
(FRENCH BELL PEPPER STEW)

Caroline Randall Williams

This summertime stew of peppers and tomatoes cooked down to their essence makes for a sunny breakfast when topped with a poached egg or two. Caroline, author of the cookbook *Soul Food Love* and an artist in residence at Nashville's Fisk University, discovered *pipérade* as a child while visiting her godmother in Sorde-l'Abbaye, a village in southwestern France. "The first time she made *pipérade*, served with a curl of country ham and an egg, it was a revelation. I asked for thirds," Caroline says. Surprisingly, this recipe did not come from Caroline's massive cookbook collection—two thousand volumes that she inherited from her trailblazing grandmother Joan Bontemps Williams—but from her godmother's neighbors. Their advice? "Cook gently."

Makes 4 to 6 servings

2 tablespoons olive oil
2 yellow onions, thinly sliced
4 bell peppers, cut into slivers
6 tomatoes
**1½ teaspoons kosher salt, plus more
   as needed**
Freshly ground black pepper
Pinch of sugar (optional)

Heat the oil in a Dutch oven or large pot over medium-low heat. Add the onion and cook, stirring occasionally, for 15 to 20 minutes. Add the bell peppers and reduce the heat to low. Cook, stirring occasionally, until the peppers begin to soften, 15 to 20 minutes.

Meanwhile, set a pot of water to boil and prepare a bowl of ice water. Once the water has begun to boil, drop in the tomatoes and cook for about 45 seconds, or until their skins begin to pucker and tear. Remove the tomatoes with a slotted spoon and plunge them into the ice water. Peel, seed, and coarsely chop the tomatoes.

Add the tomatoes to the onion and pepper mixture. Season with the salt and black pepper to taste. Taste the mixture for seasoning and if necessary, add more salt or cut the acidity with a pinch of sugar.

Cook the mixture over low heat, stirring occasionally, for about 1½ hours, until it becomes thick and stew-like and much of the liquid has evaporated. Serve as a spread or a condiment, or with ham and eggs like Caroline's godmother.

SINUGLAW
(FILIPINO GRILLED PORK BELLY & TUNA CEVICHE)

Yana Gilbuena

Here you have a delicious coming together of two popular techniques in Filipino cuisine: *sugba*, or grilling, and *kinilaw*, cooking with vinegar or citric acid. "*Sinuglaw* combines two things I love the most: raw fish and marinated pork belly," says Yana. "It's the perfect surf and turf." This "gypsy chef," as she calls herself, wanted everyone to love Filipino food as much as she does, so she quit her day job, hit the road, and produced Filipino pop-up dinners in all fifty states. Now she's hosting Filipino dinners around the world.

Make the pork belly: Combine the soy sauce, calamansi juice, sugar, pepper, and chili oil in a large bowl. Add the pork belly to the mixture and marinate in the refrigerator for 1 to 2 hours.

Light a grill. (No grill? See Tip.) Once hot, grill the pork belly for 2 to 3 minutes per side, basting with the marinade. The pork belly is done when it is browned and nicely charred. Cut into ½-inch pieces and set aside.

Make the tuna: In a glass bowl or other nonreactive container, combine the tuna, vinegar, chiles, ginger, and onion. Sprinkle the lime leaves on top. Cover and refrigerate for 1 to 2 hours.

Drain and discard the liquid, reserving all the other ingredients. Add the coconut milk and mix well to coat the fish. In a separate bowl, combine the cherry tomatoes, sesame oil, and salt.

To serve, mix the tuna with the cherry tomatoes, top with the pork belly, and sprinkle with lemon zest.

Makes 6 servings

Pork Belly
½ cup soy sauce
¼ cup calamansi juice,
    or 2 tablespoons lemon and
    2 tablespoons lime juice
¼ cup packed dark brown sugar
½ tablespoon freshly ground
    black pepper
1 tablespoon chili oil
1 pound pork belly, sliced
    lengthwise ¼ inch thick

Tuna
1 pound fresh tuna, cubed
1¼ cups cane, distilled white,
    or coconut vinegar
8 pieces chopped fresh Thai
    or bird's-eye chile (or less
    depending on preference)
2 tablespoons diced fresh ginger
1 medium red onion, diced
4 to 6 kaffir lime leaves, cut into
    thin strips
1 cup coconut milk
1 cup cherry tomatoes, halved
2 teaspoons sesame oil
1 teaspoon kosher or coarse sea salt

Zest of 1 lemon, for serving

Tip: You can bake the pork belly. Preheat the oven to 350°F, put the pork and the marinade in an oven-safe dish, cover, and bake for 20 to 30 minutes.

ZUCCHINI FARCIES
WITH YOGURT SAUCE

Laila Gohar

A food designer and artist raised in Cairo, Laila is known for creating unique feasts and edible installations for clients in the fashion, beauty, and art worlds. However, this light vegetarian dish featuring zucchini that's been hollowed out, stuffed, cooked in a tomato broth, and drizzled with a tangy yogurt sauce is more indicative of the food Laila enjoys during her downtime. She learned how to make this recipe from her mother, who is of Turkish descent, and who learned it from her own mother. Where does Laila's inventive side come from? Her dad. While her mom specialized in fare such as this, her dad cooked up crazier things, like fish-and-strawberry mousse.

Makes 8 to 10 servings

5 medium zucchini
½ medium onion, minced
2 garlic cloves, minced
1 cup short-grain rice
¾ teaspoon kosher salt
½ teaspoon ground allspice
½ teaspoon ground cinnamon
1 teaspoon ground cumin
1 tablespoon dried mint, crushed
  with your fingertips
2 tablespoons tomato paste
2 cups boiling water
1 tablespoon olive oil
Freshly ground black pepper
Yogurt Sauce (recipe follows),
  for drizzling
2 tablespoons chopped fresh basil
  (optional)
1 tablespoon fresh thyme leaves
  (optional)

Preheat the oven to 350°F.

Slice each zucchini in half crosswise, leaving the ends intact. Gently hollow out each piece using a melon baller or a teaspoon measuring spoon, putting the scooped-out flesh in a bowl as you work. Set the zucchini halves to the side. Add the minced onion and 1 minced garlic clove to the bowl and mix. Layer the mixture in the bottom of a roasting pan that can accommodate all 10 zucchini halves.

In a separate bowl, combine the rice, the remaining garlic, ¼ teaspoon of the salt, the allspice, cinnamon, cumin, and mint. Add a teaspoon or two of water and mix so that the dry spices adhere to the dry rice. Using a spoon and your fingers, stuff each hollow zucchini halfway with the rice mixture. Do not overstuff, as the rice will expand while cooking.

Combine the tomato paste with the boiling water and the remaining ½ teaspoon salt.

Nestle the zucchini pieces in the baking dish and pour the tomato water into the pan. Drizzle with the olive oil and season with pepper. Cover with aluminum foil and bake for 1 hour, or until the rice is cooked and the zucchini has softened.

To serve, drizzle the zucchini with the yogurt sauce and garnish with the basil and thyme, if desired.

YOGURT SAUCE

Makes about ½ cup

½ cup plain Greek yogurt
1 garlic clove, minced
Juice of ½ lemon
1 tablespoon dried mint,
  crushed with your fingertips
¼ teaspoon kosher salt

Combine the yogurt, garlic, lemon juice, mint, salt, and ¼ cup water in a small bowl. Stir until smooth.

RAMP FRIED RICE

Jennifer Rubell

This crispy, crunchy dish is the perfect vehicle for ramps, the wild leeks available only in the spring and prized for their pungent bite. Jennifer, a conceptual artist who often uses food as a medium, as with her "Padded Cell" installation made of cotton candy and her "Faith" meditation on fertility via egg custard tarts, says there's nothing high concept about this dish: she simply had some leftover rice in her refrigerator and wanted to use it up. Jennifer promises the more you make this, the better your technique will become. But don't delay. Art is eternal, but ramp season is short.

Makes 2 servings

2 tablespoons olive oil
3 cups cold cooked short grain brown rice
1 bunch ramps, trimmed, and cut into 1-inch pieces
¼ teaspoon sea salt

Heat a 10-inch cast-iron or heavy-bottomed pan over high heat. Add the olive oil, then the rice. Press down on the rice with the back of a spatula and spread it around the pan until flat. After a few minutes, break up the rice, add the ramps, stir, and flatten again. Repeat the break-stir-flatten process every few minutes for approximately 10 minutes.

To finish, lightly press down on the rice with the spatula and cook for 2 minutes more, until a crust forms. Flip the entire circle (or flip in two pieces if that's easier) so the crust is on top. Turn off the heat. Sprinkle with the sea salt, allow to cool, and serve straight from the pan.

WHEAT BERRY STEW
WITH ASPARAGUS & PARMESAN

Katie Baldwin & Amanda Merrow

Katie and Amanda love this recipe because wheat just happens to be the signature crop at their Long Island farm, Amber Waves. Like many farmers, they have a community supported agriculture (CSA) program and often include nutty wheat berries as part of the weekly offering. When members ask how to cook the kernels, Katie and Amanda often suggest this preparation, which is inspired by risotto. It's adaptable based on the season, so try asparagus in the spring, corn and cherry tomatoes in the summer, sweet potato and kale in the fall, and roasted squash in the winter.

Makes 4 servings

Kosher salt

1½ cups hard red wheat berries

1 tablespoon olive oil

2 garlic cloves, smashed

¼ teaspoon crushed red pepper flakes

½ medium onion, diced

½ cup dry white wine

½ bunch asparagus, ends trimmed and cut into 2-inch pieces

1 cup vegetable or chicken stock

1 teaspoon arrowroot powder or cornstarch

½ cup grated Parmigiano-Reggiano cheese, plus more for finishing

Freshly ground black pepper

2 tablespoons chopped fresh flat-leaf parsley

Bring 4 cups lightly salted water to a boil in a medium pot. Add the wheat berries, cover, and reduce the heat to medium-low. Simmer until the grains are soft and cooked through, about 1 to 1½ hours. Remove from the heat and drain any excess liquid.

Heat the olive oil, garlic, and red pepper flakes in a large skillet over low heat to infuse the oil with garlic flavor. Cook slowly over low heat for 5 minutes, until fragrant. Remove and discard the garlic cloves. Add the onion to the skillet. Season with salt. Increase the heat to medium and cook for about 5 minutes, until the onion is translucent. Add the wine and simmer for 3 to 5 minutes, until the liquid has reduced by half.

Add the wheat berries, asparagus, and stock and cook for about 5 minutes, until the asparagus is crisp-tender.

In a small bowl, combine the arrowroot with 1 tablespoon water, whisking until smooth. Stir into the pan and allow the sauce to thicken, 1 to 2 minutes. Stir in the cheese and season with salt and pepper.

Divide the stew among four bowls. Garnish each dish with additional cheese and the parsley. Serve immediately.

Tip: Hard red wheat berries have the outer hull intact, so they take longer to cook and are chewier than soft or white wheat berries. You can cook the red wheat berries for longer than recommended above, and with more water, for a fluffier result. Also, you can substitute soft or white berries, but note that they cook much faster.

SWEET POTATO WEDGES
WITH TAHINI & SCALLIONS

Vivian Howard

Think of this as a contemporary take on a very Southern ingredient. Vivian, the chef behind the Peabody Award–winning reality series *A Chef's Life,* turns the humble tuber into a fantastic side dish by roasting thick wedges and drizzling them with a honey-kissed tahini sauce and fresh herbs. Updated Southern cuisine has become a trademark of Vivian's, both on her show and at Chef & The Farmer, the celebrated restaurant she opened in her hometown of Kinston, North Carolina. This recipe perfectly illustrates the coming together of old and new she loves so much.

Makes 2 servings

1 large sweet potato
2 tablespoons olive oil
Kosher salt
3 tablespoons tahini
2 tablespoons honey
Juice of 1 lemon
1 teaspoon toasted sesame oil
2 teaspoons sesame seeds
2 tablespoons thinly sliced scallion (green part only)
¼ cup chopped fresh cilantro
¼ cup chopped fresh mint

Preheat the oven to 400°F.

Cut the potato into 8 wedges, leaving the skin intact. Toss the wedges with the olive oil and ½ teaspoon salt in a shallow bowl or pan with your hands to coat the wedges evenly. Arrange the wedges on a baking sheet, flesh-side down and not touching.

Roast for 15 minutes, then flip the potatoes over and roast for 10 minutes more, or until the potatoes are browned on all sides and creamy in the center.

Meanwhile, in a small bowl, whisk together the tahini, honey, lemon juice, sesame oil, and ¼ teaspoon salt. If the dressing seems too thick, whisk in a little water to loosen it up. When the potatoes are done, arrange them in a single layer on a serving platter and drizzle liberally with the tahini dressing. Sprinkle with the sesame seeds, scallion, cilantro, and mint and serve at room temperature.

THREE-CHEESE CAULIFLOWER GRATIN

Anna Weinberg

Anna, the restaurateur behind San Francisco's Park Tavern, The Marlowe, Leo's Oyster Bar, and The Cavalier, grew up with a mom who wasn't the greatest in the kitchen. But young Anna did love her mother's signature creation—cauliflower casserole. When Anna opened The Marlowe, she worked with Chef Jennifer Puccio to elevate her mother's classic to a new level of deliciousness and this golden, buttery gratin was born. A trio of cheeses—provolone, smoked cheddar, and traditional cheddar—and a bit of Dijon mustard turn the cauliflower into a sumptuous side dish.

Makes 6 servings

Kosher salt

4 bay leaves

1½ teaspoons whole black peppercorns

1 head cauliflower (about 3 pounds), cut into large florets

4 tablespoons (½ stick) unsalted butter

1 tablespoon Dijon mustard

3 tablespoons all-purpose flour

1 cup whole milk

1 cup heavy cream

2 cups shredded mixed cheeses (provolone, smoked cheddar, and/or medium cheddar), plus more to finish

Freshly ground black pepper

Smoked sea salt, for finishing (optional)

Bring some salted water to a boil in a large stockpot. Add the bay leaves and peppercorns. Blanch the cauliflower florets for 4 minutes, until tender but firm. Drain and rinse under cold water. Discard the bay leaves and peppercorns and set the florets aside in a large bowl.

Preheat the oven to 400°F.

Melt the butter with the Dijon mustard in a medium saucepan over low heat. Cook for 1 to 2 minutes, allowing the mixture to brown slightly. Add the flour and cook, stirring continuously with a wooden spoon, for 2 minutes. Working gradually, whisk in the milk and the cream. Increase the heat to medium, bring to a boil, then remove from the heat and stir in the cheese. Pour over the cauliflower and gently toss to combine. Season with some salt and pepper.

Fill a 10-inch cast-iron skillet with the cauliflower mixture, top with additional cheese, and bake for 20 to 25 minutes, until the top is browned. Put a baking sheet on the rack underneath the skillet to catch any cheese that might bubble over. Remove from the oven, finish with the smoked salt, if desired, and serve.

BUTTERED CHANTERELLES

Iliana Regan

There's something magical about chanterelles. The mushrooms have a golden glow and when sautéed, emit an incredible fragrance—unlike any food you've ever smelled before. It's no surprise these fungi are favored by Iliana, the chef behind the celebrated Chicago restaurant Elizabeth. As a child, Iliana picked chanterelles on her grandfather's farm and learned how to cook them from her father. She now serves them, along with other ingredients she's foraged, on her tasting menu, which takes inspiration from fairy tales, *Game of Thrones*, and other enchanted stories. These chanterelles make a beautiful side dish for a special-occasion meal.

1 pound chanterelles
1 tablespoon canola oil
Kosher salt
1 teaspoon granulated sugar
2 teaspoons red wine vinegar
1½ tablespoons unsalted butter
Freshly ground black pepper
1 teaspoon fresh thyme leaves,
  for garnish

Brush any dirt off the chanterelles or quickly swish them under water to clean if necessary. If rinsed, let the chanterelles dry for 10 minutes on a dishtowel. Any large chanterelles should be cut lengthwise into smaller pieces. Trim away any dry or unsightly pieces.

Heat the canola oil over medium heat in a sauté pan large enough to hold the mushrooms without crowding them. Stir in the chanterelles and ⅛ teaspoon salt. Cook until the liquid released by the mushrooms has evaporated and the mushrooms are slightly browned around the edges, 5 to 7 minutes.

Sprinkle in the sugar and the vinegar and stir. Add the butter, another ⅛ teaspoon salt, and some pepper. Stir to prevent the butter from becoming too hot and separating. When the butter has coated the mushrooms and cooked away a bit, remove the pan from the heat. Taste for seasoning.

Garnish with the thyme leaves and serve warm.

PUMPKIN-SWIRLED MASHED POTATOES
WITH VEGAN ROSEMARY GRAVY

Chloe Coscarelli

These fluffy potatoes, streaked with golden pumpkin purée and served with a side of creamy gravy, are a feast for the eyes and the taste buds—and it's all vegan. That's because Chloe, the celebrated vegan chef and cookbook author, has been cooking this way since her teenage years. She first made this side dish when she and her mother catered her brother's wedding. (Veganism is a family affair for the Coscarellis.) "This garnered all the praise—even more so than the cake!"

Makes 4 to 6 servings

- 3 russet potatoes, peeled and cut into 2-inch pieces
- Kosher salt
- 1 (15-ounce) can pumpkin purée
- ¼ cup packed light brown sugar
- ¾ cup low-sodium vegetable stock or unsweetened almond milk
- 3 tablespoons olive oil
- ½ teaspoon sea salt, plus more as needed
- Freshly ground black pepper
- Vegan Rosemary Gravy (recipe follows), for serving

Place the potatoes in a large pot and cover with cold water. Generously salt the water, cover, and bring to a boil. Reduce to a simmer and cook until the potatoes are fork-tender, about 20 minutes.

Cook the pumpkin purée and brown sugar in a small saucepan over medium heat until the sugar has dissolved and the pumpkin is warm. Set aside and keep warm.

Drain the potatoes and return them to the pot. Add ½ cup of the stock and the olive oil and mash everything together. Stir in the salt and season with pepper. Taste for seasoning and consistency and add more stock and salt if necessary.

Transfer the potatoes to a serving bowl. Gently swirl in the pumpkin mixture, being careful not to combine the two completely. Serve immediately with the rosemary gravy, or cover and keep warm until ready to serve.

VEGAN ROSEMARY GRAVY

Makes about 2 cups

- 3 tablespoons olive oil
- ⅓ cup all-purpose flour
- 2 tablespoons nutritional yeast
- 2 cups low-sodium vegetable stock
- 2 teaspoons chopped fresh rosemary leaves
- 1 tablespoon tamari
- ¼ teaspoon sea salt
- Freshly ground black pepper

Warm the olive oil in a medium saucepan over medium heat. Add the flour and nutritional yeast and cook, whisking continuously, until the flour just begins to brown. The mixture will be crumbly.

Slowly add the stock, rosemary, and tamari and cook, whisking continuously, until the gravy thickens and no lumps remain. Add the salt and some pepper. If the gravy is too thick, add water 1 tablespoon at a time until the desired consistency is achieved. Serve immediately, or keep warm until ready to serve.

JOAN TISHGART'S NOODLE KUGEL

Sierra Tishgart

A staple of Jewish cooking, kugel is a noodle casserole that's sweet instead of savory. Sierra, senior editor of *New York* magazine's *Grub Street* and an authority on the city's restaurant scene, couldn't imagine Thanksgiving without it. "To my mom's dismay, as soon as the kugel comes out of the oven, I have to sneak a taste. There's always a corner missing when she sets it out on the table," says Sierra. "It tastes like home."

Makes one 9 × 13-inch pan (10 servings)

Unsalted butter, for greasing the pan
8 ounces medium egg noodles
¾ pound cream cheese, at room
    temperature
1 cup granulated sugar
4 large eggs
1 (12-ounce) can evaporated milk
2 cups whole milk
¾ cup golden raisins
¼ teaspoon ground cinnamon,
    for serving
1 pint sour cream,
    for serving (optional)

Grease a 9 × 13-inch casserole dish with butter. Bring a large pot of water to a boil and add the noodles. Cook according to the package instructions until al dente, then drain and set aside.

In a large bowl, combine the cream cheese and sugar. Mix in the eggs, evaporated milk, and whole milk.

Put the noodles in the prepared casserole dish and pour the liquid mixture over the top. Sprinkle the raisins across the surface and gently push them below the liquid. Refrigerate the casserole for a few hours or up to overnight before baking.

Preheat the oven to 350°F.

Bake the casserole for 1 hour, or until the kugel sets, the top is golden, and the edges have begun to brown. The top will puff up slightly, but deflate once cool. Sprinkle with cinnamon and, if desired, add a dollop of sour cream before serving.

APPS, SNACKS & SIPS

GARNET YAM PANCAKES
WITH CRÈME FRAÎCHE & CAVIAR

Tanya Holland

These sweet, savory, bite-size hors d'oeuvres will steal all the attention at your next gathering. They're delicious unadorned, but the crème fraîche and caviar transform them into next-level treats. Brown Sugar Kitchen's community-minded chef/owner Tanya Holland knows a lot about making guests happy. Fans return to her Oakland spot again and again for her hospitality and comfort food classics, such as buttermilk fried chicken with cornmeal waffles and BBQ shrimp and grits. Once your friends taste these pancakes, be prepared for a crowd in your kitchen.

Makes about 50 small pancakes

1 large yellow onion, halved
3 organic red garnet yams
   (1¾ to 2 pounds), peeled
1 cup all-purpose flour
1¼ teaspoons baking powder
1½ teaspoons kosher salt
Freshly ground black pepper
3 large eggs
3 tablespoons unsalted butter,
   melted
Canola oil, for frying
Crème fraîche, for serving
1 (1- to 2-ounce) tin caviar
   (optional; see Tip)

Line a large colander with a dishtowel or a double layer of cheesecloth. Shred the onion halves on a box grater into the colander. (Or use a food processor or a stand mixer fitted with the shredding attachment.) Gather the corners of the towel and wring out as much excess liquid as you can. Shred the yams into the lined colander. Toss the shredded yam with the onions. Let sit for 5 minutes, then repeat with the wringing to remove as much liquid as possible from the yam and onion.

In a large bowl, whisk together the flour, baking powder, salt, and pepper. In another bowl, whisk together the eggs and butter, then combine the dry and wet mixtures. Add the yam-onion mixture and stir until well combined and evenly coated.

Heat ¼ inch of canola oil in a large heavy skillet over medium heat. Measure a packed tablespoonful of the yam-onion mixture, add it to the skillet, and lightly press with a spatula to flatten. Repeat until the pan is full, taking care not to overcrowd the pan. Cook, turning once, until just golden, about 4 minutes total. Transfer to a baking sheet, plate, or rack lined with paper towels. Keep warm in the oven set on low. Repeat with the remaining batter.

Top the pancakes with a dollop of crème fraîche and a little bit of caviar, if desired, before serving.

The pancakes can be made the day before serving. Let cool to room temperature on a wire rack, then transfer to a baking sheet. Wrap the sheet tightly with plastic wrap and refrigerate. Reheat the pancakes on a baking sheet in a preheated 400°F oven for 10 to 15 minutes or in a dry skillet.

Tip: A little bit of caviar goes a long way in this case. To make this less of a splurge, look for the more affordable American caviar and be sure to choose a brand that's sustainably harvested.

GOAT CHEESE SOUFFLÉS

Louisa Conrad

The herbaceous tang of goat cheese is present in every bite of these airy mini soufflés. Chives, cayenne, and nutmeg balance the bold taste of the cheese. For Louisa, this recipe, based on a classic by Alice Waters, is a great way to use everything she has on hand at Big Picture Farm, the Vermont property where she and her husband tend to a much-loved herd of goats. Big Picture produces award-winning cheeses and caramels and Louisa, an artist, illustrates the packaging. She recommends serving the soufflés alongside greens and radishes, a spicy, clean contrast to the richness.

Makes 8 small soufflés

3 tablespoons unsalted butter, plus more for the ramekins
¼ cup goat's-milk Parmesan (or regular Parmesan), grated, for dusting the ramekins
2 tablespoons all-purpose flour
½ cup goat's milk (or cow's milk)
¼ teaspoon freshly grated nutmeg
⅛ teaspoon cayenne pepper
Kosher salt and freshly ground black pepper
4 large eggs, separated
4 ounces soft goat cheese, crumbled
3 tablespoons finely chopped fresh chives

Preheat the oven to 400°F.

Butter eight small (4-ounce) ramekins and dust lightly with the Parmesan. Place on a baking sheet, 2 inches apart.

Melt the butter in a small saucepan over medium heat. Add the flour and whisk for 2 minutes, until smooth. Gradually whisk in the milk. Be sure to whisk thoroughly between each addition to avoid lumps. Season with the nutmeg, cayenne, and pinches of salt and pepper. Cook over low heat, stirring occasionally, for 5 minutes.

Using a whisk, stir in the egg yolks, then add the soft goat cheese and whisk until smooth. Remove from the heat, add the chives, and stir well to combine. Transfer to a large bowl and set aside.

In the bowl of a stand mixer fitted with the whisk attachment, whip the egg whites on medium speed until they hold firm peaks, 1 to 2 minutes. With a rubber spatula, gently fold one-third of the whites into the goat cheese base. Gently fold in the remainder of the egg whites, working carefully so as not to deflate them.

Pour the mixture into the prepared ramekins, leaving room at the top of each for the soufflé to rise. Bake for 20 minutes, or until fluffy, golden, and slightly jiggly. Do not open the oven door while baking or the soufflés might fall. Serve immediately.

GOUGÈRES

Melanie Dunea

There's a reason so many chefs serve *gougères* as an amuse-bouche. Nothing makes guests happier than these warm puffs of cheesy goodness, and they're easier to make than you would guess. Melanie, a globetrotting photographer and the creator of the *My Last Supper* series of books, was introduced to them while shooting the great French chef Alain Ducasse. "I adapted his recipe and added even more cheese," she notes. "He would probably say I Americanized it!" Her number one tip? "Always serve with Champagne."

Makes about 40 gougères

½ cup whole milk
½ cup (1 stick) unsalted butter, cut into tablespoons
½ teaspoon kosher salt
1 cup all-purpose flour
4 large eggs
1½ cups shredded Gruyère cheese, plus ¼ cup for sprinkling
¼ teaspoon freshly grated nutmeg
Freshly ground black pepper

Preheat the oven to 375°F.

Combine ½ cup water, the milk, butter, and salt in a medium saucepan and bring to a boil. Add the flour a bit at a time, stirring with a wooden spoon until a smooth dough forms. Cook, stirring, until the dough pulls away from the pan, about 2 minutes.

Transfer the dough to a bowl and let cool, about 1 minute. Beat 1 egg at a time into the dough, incorporating thoroughly. Add the cheese, nutmeg, and some pepper.

Line two baking sheets with parchment paper. Fit a pastry bag with a ½-inch tip, fill the bag with the batter, and pipe 1-inch mounds onto the baking sheet, 1 inch apart. (If you don't have a pastry bag, use a spoon. You can wet your fingers slightly and smooth down any jagged bits of dough.) Sprinkle with the remaining cheese and bake for 20 to 22 minutes, until puffed and slightly golden. Do not overcook and do not let them brown. Repeat the process with any remaining batter. Serve while warm.

The *gougères* can be made ahead of time. Once they cool, freeze in a sealed bag or container. Reheat the puffs in a 350°F oven for 10 to 15 minutes.

GRILLED OYSTERS
WITH GREMOLATA & CHILI BUTTER

Ashley Christensen

The garlicky gremolata sets off the smoky richness of the oysters and the butter in this crave-worthy appetizer from Ashley, the chef behind seven bustling establishments in Raleigh, North Carolina. Ashley loves oysters and grilling, so this recipe lets her play around with some of her favorite things. These amped-up oysters also happen to be one of the most popular menu items at her restaurant Death & Taxes, so when she suggests doubling the recipe, you might want to listen. "Make more than you think you need," she says. "People always grab these up!" If you don't have a grill, you can broil the oysters in your oven.

Make the gremolata: Remove the rind from the preserved lemon, being careful not to include the white pith. Finely dice the rind and discard the pith.

Put the garlic, parsley, and lemon juice in a food processor and pulse until finely chopped. With the motor running, slowly drizzle in the olive oil. Transfer to a small bowl and fold in the diced preserved lemon rind. Stir in the salt and taste for seasoning.

Make the oysters: Light a charcoal grill, removing the main grill grate. (Or, if broiling, set your oven to broil.)

In a medium bowl, combine the butter, lemon zest, lemon juice, and chili paste with a fork until smooth. Set aside.

Line a grill basket (or a baking sheet, if you are broiling) with rock salt or crumpled aluminum foil. Arrange the oysters in an even layer in the basket (work in batches if necessary), being careful not to tip them over and lose their juices. Top each oyster with about 1 teaspoon of the butter. Place the basket directly in the embers and roast for 5 minutes or until the butter is melted and starts to boil and the oysters are slightly rippled.

Remove the oysters from the heat, transfer to a platter, and top each with ½ teaspoon of the gremolata. Serve warm.

Makes 24 oysters

Gremolata
½ preserved lemon
½ garlic clove, coarsely chopped
1 bunch fresh flat-leaf parsley, or 1 packed cup fresh flat-leaf parsley leaves
Juice of ½ lemon
¼ cup olive oil
¼ teaspoon fine sea salt, plus more as needed

Oysters
½ cup (1 stick) unsalted butter, at room temperature
Zest and juice of ½ lemon
½ teaspoon chili paste or sambal
Rock salt
24 medium oysters, shucked, on the half shell

MOM'S RETRO CUCUMBER SANDWICHES

Jamie Malone

While working at the acclaimed Sea Change in Minneapolis, Jamie earned a reputation for her clean, updated cuisine. But this serious chef has a soft spot for her mom's retro recipes for everything from mini hot dogs in grape jelly sauce to these open-faced cucumber sandwiches. "My mom is amazing and brilliant, but aside from her repertoire of 1970s kitsch dishes, she does not have a reputation for being a great cook," says Jamie. "She is getting more into cooking now and making new things, but the whole family is like, 'NOOOOO! Where are the cocktail weenies?'"

1 package rye cocktail bread or 12 pieces regular rye bread
8 ounces cream cheese, at room temperature
½ packet dry Italian seasoning
¼ cup chopped fresh dill, plus more for garnish
2 English cucumbers, cut into ¼-inch-thick slices (and peeled, if desired)
1 tablespoon olive oil
½ tablespoon fresh lemon juice
Flaky sea salt

Preheat the oven to 350°F.

Arrange 24 slices of the cocktail rye bread on a baking sheet. (If using regular rye bread, cut each slice in half.) Lightly toast for 3 minutes. Flip and toast for 2 minutes more.

In a medium bowl, mix the cream cheese, Italian seasoning, and dill. In another bowl, toss the cucumbers with the olive oil and lemon juice.

Move the toast to a platter. Spread each piece with some cream cheese and top with 1 or 2 cucumber slices. Sprinkle with sea salt, garnish with dill, and serve.

LATKES
WITH PEAR SAUCE

Jenn Louis

This Portland, Oregon–based chef/owner of Ray restaurant tweaked her mother's Hanukkah recipe to come up with potato latkes that strike "the perfect balance between being pillowy and thick and thin and crispy." Jenn updates the family tradition even further by topping them with a pear sauce that's been lightly sweetened with apple cider. "Growing up, we would eat them with applesauce and sour cream, the same way my Ashkenazi family would eat them in Poland and Russia before they came to the United States. I keep the foods we celebrated with near and dear to my heart."

Makes 24 small pancakes

1½ pounds Yukon Gold potatoes
Kosher salt
1 medium yellow onion
2 tablespoons all-purpose flour
3 tablespoons matzo meal
Freshly ground black pepper
2 large eggs
1 cup canola oil
Sour cream or plain Greek yogurt,
    for serving
Pear Sauce (recipe follows),
    for serving

Preheat the oven to 350°F.

Peel the potatoes, then shred them on the large holes of a box grater set over a large bowl. Mix in ½ teaspoon salt and let the potatoes rest while you grate the onion on the box grater into another bowl. Place the shredded potatoes in a clean dishtowel and wring out the excess moisture over the sink. Add the potatoes in the bowl with the onion and add the flour, matzo meal, ½ teaspoon salt, some pepper, and the eggs. Mix well without kneading.

Place two layers of paper towels on a baking sheet. Heat the canola oil in a large skillet until it shimmers. Form the potato mixture into 2-inch patties and, working in batches, fry until golden on the first side, about 2 minutes. Flip and fry for another minute or two, being careful not to let them get too brown, then transfer them to the paper towels to drain. Repeat with the rest of the mixture. Season all the latkes with ½ teaspoon salt.

Remove the paper towels from the baking sheet and bake the latkes for 10 minutes. Serve immediately with sour cream and pear sauce.

PEAR SAUCE

Makes 1½ to 2 cups

5 pears, peeled, cored, and cut
    into 1-inch pieces
1 cup apple cider
1 vanilla bean
¼ teaspoon freshly grated nutmeg
⅓ teaspoon orange zest
¼ teaspoon kosher salt

In a large pot, combine the pears and cider. Scrape the vanilla bean seeds into the pot, then add the pod. Simmer over medium heat until the pears are soft. Remove the pears with a slotted spoon and set them aside, leaving the liquid behind. Cook the liquid over medium heat until syrupy, 10 to 15 minutes.

Remove and discard the vanilla pod. Process the pears in a food processor until smooth, then add the syrup, nutmeg, orange zest, and the salt and pulse until combined.

When ready to use, warm the pear sauce in a small saucepan. The pear sauce will keep in an airtight container in the refrigerator for up to 3 days.

ROTI PIZZA PARTY

Priya Krishna

Priya's mom, who moved to the States from India, would make traditional vegetarian fare almost every night of the week for her family. When Priya and her sister clamored for "American" food, their resourceful mother came up with a mix-and-match "pizza" night, using whatever was in the refrigerator—rotis, vegetables, cheese, and herbs. It's no wonder Priya grew up to write a cookbook called *Ultimate Dining Hall Hacks*, based on her experiences jazzing up the food at her college cafeteria. If you're throwing your own roti pizza party, feel free to play around with the toppings. Just don't skip the prebaking step, cautions Priya. The crispy crust is key.

ROTI PIZZA CRUST

Makes 2 pizzas

2 (9-inch) rotis, whole wheat tortillas, or flatbreads
2 teaspoons olive oil
½ teaspoon sea salt

Preheat the oven to 400°F.

Score each roti a few times with a knife to prevent it from puffing up. Place on a perforated pizza pan (or a broiler pan). Drizzle 1 teaspoon of the olive oil on each roti and smooth it across the surface with your fingers. Sprinkle each with ¼ teaspoon of the sea salt. Bake for 5 minutes. Remove and follow the directions below for the toppings of your choice.

POTATO & ROSEMARY TOPPING

1 medium potato, very thinly sliced
1 tablespoon coarsely chopped fresh rosemary
½ teaspoon sea salt
1 cup grated Parmigiano-Reggiano cheese
2 teaspoons olive oil

Layer the potato slices on the crispy rotis. Sprinkle each roti with ½ tablespoon rosemary and ¼ teaspoon salt. Bake for 5 minutes.

Remove from the oven and sprinkle ½ cup of the cheese on each pizza. Bake for 5 minutes more. To serve, drizzle each pizza with 1 teaspoon of the olive oil and cut into quarters.

FETA, ONION & TOMATO TOPPING

1 large or 2 medium tomatoes
2 small garlic cloves, chopped
¼ medium red onion, thinly sliced
3 to 4 long strips feta cheese (use the kind that comes in a block)
2 teaspoons olive oil
1 tablespoon halved Kalamata olives or drained capers

Remove and discard the seeds and core of the tomato. Cut the tomato into matchstick-size slivers. Dry the slivers and add to a bowl with the garlic. Set aside for 15 to 20 minutes to allow the flavors to meld.

Layer the tomato, garlic, and onions on the crispy rotis. Bake for 5 minutes. Add the feta cheese and bake for 5 minutes more.

To serve, drizzle each pizza with 1 teaspoon of the olive oil, sprinkle with the olives, and cut into quarters.

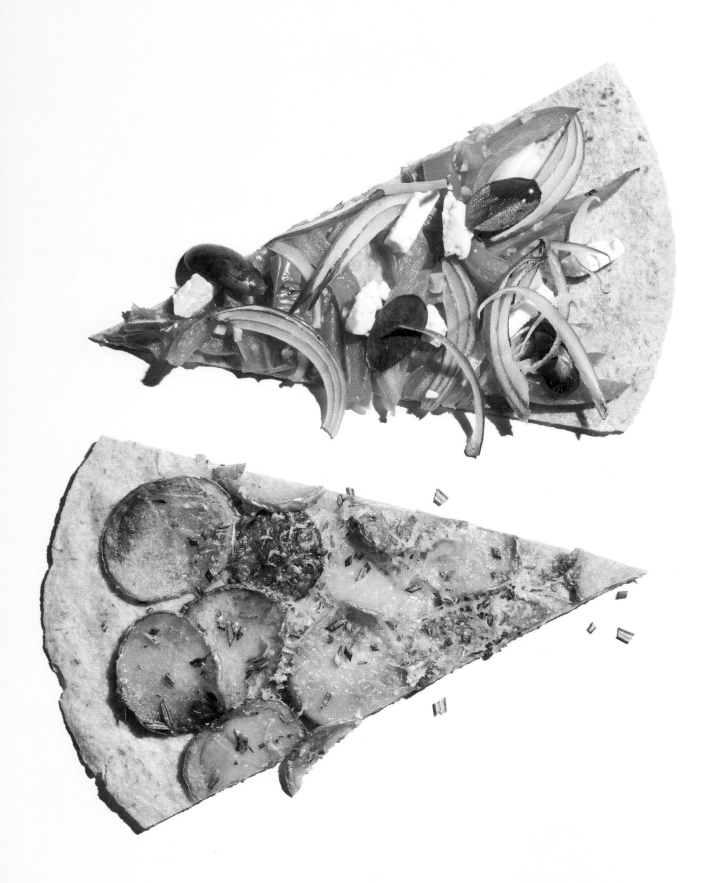

POGACA
(SAVORY TURKISH PASTRIES)

Naz Sahin Ozcan

These warm Middle Eastern treats represent a taste of home for Naz, who writes and illustrates the "Mixed Nuts" feature on food history and culture in each issue of *Cherry Bombe*. Traditionally, *pogaca* are stuffed with ground beef or a type of cheese known as *beyaz peynir* (more similar to a creamy French feta than the harder, saltier Greek feta). "Step into any bakery early in the morning in Turkey and behind steamy windows you will find trays full of warm *pogaca*, waiting to be wrapped and carried to offices where they will be enjoyed with countless glasses of tea," says Naz.

Makes 30 to 40 pastries

Dough
- 4 cups all-purpose flour
- 2½ teaspoons baking powder
- 1 teaspoon kosher salt
- 1 cup (2 sticks) unsalted butter, melted
- ⅓ cup grapeseed or vegetable oil
- ½ cup whole milk
- ¾ cup full-fat plain yogurt
- 3 large eggs

Ground Beef Filling
- 1 tablespoon olive oil
- 1 small onion, finely diced
- ½ pound lean ground beef
- 1 teaspoon kosher salt
- 1 cup chopped fresh dill

Cheese Filling
- 2 cups crumbled feta cheese (Turkish or French, not Greek)
- ½ cup chopped fresh dill
- ½ cup chopped fresh flat-leaf parsley

- ¼ cup white sesame seeds
- ¼ cup nigella seeds

Make the dough: Mix the flour, baking powder, and salt in a large shallow bowl. Make a well in the center. In a medium bowl, combine the melted butter, oil, milk, and yogurt. Add 1 whole egg and the whites from the remaining 2 eggs. Set aside the yolks.

Slowly pour the mixture into the well, a bit at a time, letting it trickle into the flour, pinching the mixture with your hands as you go. When mixed, knead the dough lightly until it is smooth and soft but still sticky. Cover the bowl with a dishtowel and let the dough rest at room temperature for 20 minutes.

Make the beef filling: Heat the olive oil in a skillet over medium-low heat. Add the onion and cook gently until tender and translucent. Add the ground beef and salt. Cook gently until lightly browned, breaking it up with a wooden spoon as it cooks. Stir in the dill, remove the pan from the heat, and set aside.

Make the cheese filling: Mix the feta, dill, and parsley in a bowl and set aside.

Preheat the oven to 375°F. Line two baking sheets with parchment paper.

Pull off a small piece of dough and roll it into the shape and size of a Ping-Pong ball. Place it in the palm of one hand and tap it with the other hand to flatten the ball into a disk. Add 1 tablespoon of the beef filling to the middle of the dough, then fold the top half over the bottom half. Lightly pinch the edges and transfer to the prepared baking sheet. Repeat, making sure to leave an inch between each piece on the baking sheet. Lightly brush the tops with the reserved egg yolks and sprinkle with the sesame seeds. Repeat the steps with the cheese filling and sprinkle the nigella seeds on top.

Bake for 20 to 25 minutes, until golden. These are best eaten warm and served with tea.

STOVETOP RICOTTA

Anne Saxelby

If you've never made homemade ricotta, you will be surprised at how easy it is. Plus, whipping up a batch will give you a major sense of satisfaction, promises Anne, the founder and co-owner of Saxelby Cheesemongers in Manhattan. A champion of American farmstead cheese, Anne fell into this world after graduating from college with a fine art degree. "I feel like a lot of times you need an instruction manual to understand contemporary art. With cheese, you put it in your mouth, eat it, and can instantly judge for yourself," she says. Serve this cheese topped with a dash of good olive oil, sea salt, and cracked black pepper, and accompanied by some warm bread. Or go the sweet route and drizzle with your favorite honey, a touch of sea salt, and some fresh berries.

Makes about 4 cups

1 gallon whole milk
2 cups heavy cream
¼ teaspoon kosher salt
¾ cup fresh lemon juice
 (about 4 lemons)

Clip a thermometer to a large pot. Pour the milk and cream into the pot and season with the salt. Turn the heat to medium-high and bring the milk to 190°F. Stir often to keep the milk from scorching.

Once the milk is warm enough, turn off the heat and add the lemon juice. Stir slowly until curds and whey—clumps of cheese and a semi-clear yellowish liquid—begin to form. Let the pot of curds rest for 5 minutes.

Line a colander with cheesecloth and place it over a large bowl. Pour the curds and whey into the colander and let the curds drain for at least 1 hour. Reserve the whey for another use (see Tip).

Fresh ricotta is best consumed warm and as soon as possible, but will keep in an airtight container in the refrigerator for a few days.

Tip: Don't get rid of your whey. You can use it in Victoria Granof's Spring Greens Borscht (page 74).

LABNEH
WITH NIGELLA SEEDS & SUMAC

Homa Dashtaki

Labneh, for the uninitiated, is strained yogurt that has the consistency of cream cheese. It's tart and completely addictive. Here, Homa sprinkles it with oniony nigella seeds and lemony sumac for a taste inspired by her childhood in Tehran. Speaking of home, Homa and her dad launched their Brooklyn-based company, White Moustache, when they couldn't find anything similar to the rich, delicious yogurt they enjoyed back in Iran. This *labneh* is extra amazing because the yogurt used is homemade—by you. It's a great nighttime project, as the yogurt does its thing while you sleep. If you don't have the time or patience for homemade yogurt, you can use store-bought full-fat yogurt and skip ahead to the *labneh*-making portion of the recipe.

Makes about 4 cups

½ gallon whole milk
1½ tablespoons full-fat plain yogurt made with live active cultures
2 tablespoons olive oil
½ teaspoon whole nigella seeds
½ teaspoon ground sumac
Flaky sea salt
Pita or flatbread, for serving

About 2 hours before going to bed, place a few blankets on top of a table. Place a towel in the center of the blankets and put a ceramic bowl or Dutch oven on top of the towel.

In a large pot, bring the milk to a boil, stirring continuously. Once the milk is full of hot, frothy bubbles, turn off the heat before the liquid overflows.

Pour the milk into the bowl. Let the milk cool for 20 to 30 minutes to the point where you can hold your pinky in the liquid for 3 seconds. Add the yogurt (which acts as your starter). Cover the bowl with a lid or plate. Carefully wrap the bowl with the blankets to coddle it through the night and retain the temperature. Let it rest for 8 hours or up to overnight.

In the morning, remove the blankets and towel and refrigerate the yogurt until you're ready to make the *labneh*.

Line a large strainer with cheesecloth and set it over a large bowl. Add the fresh yogurt to the strainer and place the strainer and the bowl in the refrigerator for 10 to 14 hours. Remove the strained yogurt and transfer to a large bowl. Reserve the liquid whey for another use (such as in Victoria Granof's Spring Greens Borscht on page 74).

Drizzle the *labneh* with the olive oil and sprinkle the nigella seeds, sumac, and salt on top. Serve with the bread for dipping.

HOLY MOLY GUACAMOLE

Amirah Kassem

This classic guacamole is Amirah's favorite way to get a party started. "Everyone gathers around the guacamole at any event," she says. It's also her favorite snack and a nod to her Mexican heritage and mother, who raised Amirah in the border town of Juarez. The guac is proof that Amirah doesn't exist solely on sugar, as one might assume given her day job as boss and head baker of Flour Shop in New York City. She specializes in creative custom cakes commissioned by sweet-toothed A-listers, and Willy Wonka–inspired sweets, such as lickable wallpaper. Her kitchen tool of choice? Her imagination.

In a medium bowl, combine the onion, tomato, jalapeño, and cilantro. Scoop out the avocado flesh with a spoon and add it to the bowl. Lightly mash the avocado into the rest of the ingredients to achieve a chunky texture. Don't overmash. Add the salt and half the lime juice and stir to combine. Taste and add more salt and lime juice if necessary, a little at a time. Serve with tortilla chips.

Makes 8 servings

½ small white onion, finely chopped
1 tomato, seeded and chopped
½ jalapeño, seeded, membrane removed, and minced
1 tablespoon chopped fresh cilantro
4 ripe avocados, halved and pitted
1 teaspoon kosher salt, plus more as needed
Juice of 1 lime
Tortilla chips, for serving

MIRZA GHASEMI
(PERSIAN EGGPLANT & TOMATO SPREAD WITH EGGS)

Nilou Motamed

"I'm not sure why, but every Iranian I've ever met is crazy for eggplant," says Nilou, who was born in Tehran and today serves as editor in chief of *Food & Wine* magazine. "There's no end to the variations and preparations of aubergine in Persian cuisine, but *mirza ghasemi*, from the Gilan region of Northern Iran where my maternal grandfather was born, is among my favorites." This is her mother Mahin's tried-and-true eggplant recipe, which Nilou calls her ultimate comfort food. Here, the savory tomato-eggplant reduction, highly addictive on its own, is served with scrambled eggs. Serve as a sophisticated option for breakfast or brunch—or any time of the day.

Makes 4 servings

6 long purple Asian eggplants
  (about 2 inches in diameter)
½ cup plus 1 tablespoon olive oil
5 garlic cloves, minced
⅛ teaspoon ground turmeric
1 pound fresh tomatoes, diced
Kosher salt and freshly ground
  black pepper
4 large eggs
1 teaspoon chopped fresh chives
4 slices toasted bread (optional)

Light a grill, turn the broiler to high, or put a grill pan on your stovetop over medium-high heat.

Using a fork, poke a few holes in each eggplant. Grill or broil the eggplants, turning them a few times until they are charred all over and collapsed, 20 to 25 minutes. Transfer the eggplants to a colander set in the sink and let them cool for 10 minutes.

Peel the eggplants, being careful of the steam, and discard the skin. The pulp should be very soft. Set the pulp in the colander to drain while you cook the tomatoes.

Heat the ½ cup of olive oil in a large skillet over medium heat. Add the garlic and sauté until softened. Season with the turmeric. Add the tomatoes, ½ teaspoon salt, and some pepper and cook for 25 to 30 minutes, until the tomatoes have completely broken down and most of the liquid has evaporated.

Chop the cooled eggplant pulp and add it to the tomatoes. Cook, stirring frequently, until the oil begins to pool on the surface, 10 to 15 minutes. Blot the oil with a paper towel if you like. Taste and add more salt if necessary.

In a small bowl, whisk the eggs with a pinch each of salt and pepper. Heat the remaining 1 tablespoon olive oil in a medium nonstick skillet over medium heat. Add the eggs and cook, stirring, until just set. Shake the skillet to loosen the eggs and fold them over themselves.

Put the eggs and eggplant-tomato mixture on a platter, garnish with chives, and serve with the toast, if desired.

SALTED FLOUNDER & SWEET POTATO TARTINES

Mashama Bailey

This toast was inspired by the salt cod much loved by Mashama's Southern grandmother. Mashama uses local flounder, which she salts for twenty-four hours, poaches in milk, and transforms into a chilled salad flecked with scallions, parsley, and tiny squares of sweet potato. Think of it as the fanciest fish salad you've ever had. It's a perfect example of the food Mashama has made her trademark at The Grey in Savannah, Georgia—elevated Southern, with lots of love behind it. Her teachers over the years? They've ranged from the women in her family to Chef Gabrielle Hamilton of Manhattan's Prune restaurant, where Mashama was sous chef.

Makes 8 servings

4 flounder fillets (about 7 ounces each)
4 cups kosher salt, plus more as needed
3 cups whole milk
1 head of garlic, sliced in half lengthwise
2 dried chile de árbol
⅔ cup finely diced sweet potato
1 garlic clove, finely grated or minced
½ cup chopped scallions, green parts only
2 tablespoons chopped fresh flat-leaf parsley
½ cup mayonnaise
3 tablespoons olive oil, plus more for drizzling
Juice of 1 lemon
Freshly ground black pepper
Loaf of multigrain bread

Cover the flounder fillets in the salt and refrigerate for at least 24 hours. Remove from the salt and rinse the fillets under cold running water. Soak in cold water for at least 1 hour, changing the water five times. Remove from the water and pat dry with paper towels.

Put the milk, garlic head halves, chiles, and 1 cup water in a saucepan and bring to a simmer. Add the fish fillets and poach for 6 to 8 minutes, or until the fish becomes opaque and starts to fall apart when lifted. Put the pan in the refrigerator or in an ice bath to cool down.

Bring a small pot of salted water to a boil and cook the sweet potato for a few minutes until tender. Drain and set aside.

Using a slotted spoon, transfer the fish to a colander. Discard the poaching liquid. With a fork or your fingers, press the liquid out of the fish pieces. Flake the fish into a medium bowl and fold in the sweet potato, grated garlic, scallions, parsley, mayonnaise, olive oil, lemon juice, and a pinch each of salt and black pepper. Taste and adjust the seasoning if necessary. Chill in the refrigerator until ready to serve.

Cut the bread into 8 slices, about ½ inch thick. Toast or grill the bread. Arrange the bread on a platter and divide the flounder salad among the slices. Drizzle with a little bit of olive oil and serve.

PINK GRAPEFRUIT FIZZ

Jordan Salcito

This recipe was born one hot summer afternoon when Jordan, the wine director of the Momofuku restaurant group, was thirsting for something refreshing but sophisticated to serve her girlfriends. The cocktail she created was such a hit, it inspired her line of artisanal wine coolers called RAMONA. (Jordan, by the way, is also the founder of Bellus Wines.) The best way to serve this pretty-in-pastel drink? "With a straw, ideally on a rooftop or by a pool on a warm sunny day," says Jordan.

Makes 2 cocktails

½ cup (4 ounces) fresh pink
    grapefruit juice
¾ cup (6 ounces) dry rosé
2 tablespoons (1 ounce) Simple
    Syrup
    (recipe follows)
Crushed ice
¾ cup (6 ounces) sparkling wine or
    club soda
1 grapefruit wheel, cut in half,
    for garnish

Mix the grapefruit juice, rosé, and simple syrup together and divide between two glasses partially filled with crushed ice. Top with the sparkling wine, garnish with the grapefruit slices, and serve.

SIMPLE SYRUP

Makes about 1¼ cups

1 cup granulated sugar

In a small saucepan, combine the sugar and 1 cup water. Bring to a low boil over medium heat and stir until the sugar has dissolved, 2 to 3 minutes. Allow to cool, then transfer to a squeeze bottle or glass jar and refrigerate. The syrup will keep for up to 1 month.

CHARRED PINEAPPLE MARGARITA

Gail Simmons

This updated margarita strikes the perfect balance between sweet and smoky and tart and fresh, with an unexpected kick of cilantro. By lightly grilling the pineapple before muddling it with the fresh herbs and lime juice, Gail, the *Top Chef* judge and *Food & Wine* special projects director, gives the drink a fruit-forward twist. Speaking of Gail, she's widely considered one of the nicest people in the food biz. There's no one we'd rather hang with during happy hour.

Makes 2 cocktails

1 teaspoon canola oil
⅓ small pineapple, cored and cut into 3-inch pieces, plus 2 to 3 slices for garnish (or 1½ cups precut pineapple)
Juice of 1 lime
2 tablespoons fresh cilantro, plus more for garnish
⅓ cup (3 ounces) tequila
3 tablespoons (1½ ounces) triple sec
2 teaspoons Simple Syrup (page 156)
Ice
1 tablespoon fine salt, for garnish

Heat a grill or grill pan over medium-high heat and brush with the canola oil. Add the pineapple pieces and slices, and grill until just soft and lightly charred, 2 to 3 minutes per side. Remove from the grill and allow to cool.

Coarsely chop the pineapple pieces and transfer to a cocktail shaker along with the lime juice and cilantro leaves. Muddle everything together until the pineapple juice is extracted. Add the tequila, triple sec, simple syrup, and plenty of ice, and shake until well chilled.

Gently rub the rim of two glasses with one of the pineapple slices. Spread the salt on a plate and swirl the rim of each glass through the salt to coat. Add some ice to each glass.

Strain and divide the margarita into the glasses. Garnish each with a pineapple slice and a few cilantro leaves and serve immediately.

ROSÉ SANGRIA
WITH CHERRIES

Klancy Miller

Sangria made with our favorite pink wine, our favorite fruit, and ribbons of orange zest sounds just perfect. Klancy, the author of *Cooking Solo: The Fun of Cooking for Yourself,* created this recipe for those times when you're expecting lots of pals—for a fun brunch, lunch, or dinner party, or just hanging out. For this sangria, she prefers a full-bodied rosé, such as those from Bordeaux or a Malbec rosé from Argentina, and she uses a vegetable peeler to get the zest just right. As for the fruit, you can swap in peaches and grapes for the blueberries and nectarines. But the cherries, of course, are a must.

Makes 10 to 15 servings

3 (750-milliliter) bottles rosé, chilled
½ cup (4 ounces) brandy
2 tablespoons (1 ounce) St-Germain elderflower liqueur
Juice of ½ lime
1 cup cherries, pitted
1 or 2 ribbons orange zest
1 orange, sliced
1 nectarine, pitted and sliced
½ cup frozen blueberries
Seltzer or club soda (optional)
Ice (optional)

Pour the rosé, brandy, St-Germain, and lime juice into a large pitcher, bowl, or container. Stir with a large spoon. Add the cherries, orange zest, orange, and nectarine. Refrigerate for 1 hour so the flavors can come together. Right before serving, add the blueberries and, if desired, a splash of seltzer and some ice.

HERBAL VODKA TONIC

Lisa Q. Fetterman

When Lisa moved to America from China as a young girl with limited English skills, food became her primary language, a way for her to communicate with others and understand the culture. "Now food still speaks for me, so much more eloquently than I could have ever imagined," she says. Today, Lisa is the CEO of Nomiku, the company she founded to give amateur cooks access to the tools and techniques used in the best professional kitchens. Sometimes Lisa leaves the cooking to others, but she's always happy to mix her signature cocktail, this modern twist on a vodka tonic.

Makes 1 cocktail

Ice
3 tablespoons (1½ ounces) vodka
1 tablespoon (½ ounce) absinthe or
    other anise-flavored liqueur
2 tablespoons (1 ounce) bottled or
    fresh yuzu juice
⅓ cups (3 ounces) tonic water
Twist of lime, for garnish

Fill a Tom Collins glass with ice cubes and pour in the vodka, absinthe, yuzu, and tonic water. Stir with a bar spoon or straw, garnish with the lime, and serve immediately.

THE SINSEAR

Yvette Leeper-Bueno

Get ready to sip the perfect cold-weather concoction. The sweetness of the apple cider and the spiciness of the grated ginger mellow out the bourbon and play up its warming qualities. This was one of the first drinks on the menu at Vinatería, the Harlem restaurant owned by Yvette, and it remains a favorite of hers and her regular guests. The drink's name is derived from an old Irish term for "elder" or "ancestor," which is fitting given Yvette's affection for her neighborhood and its history.

In a cocktail shaker, combine the bourbon, cider, lemon juice, simple syrup, and ginger. Add some ice and shake. Strain into two glasses over fresh ice. Garnish each with a rosemary sprig and serve.

Makes 2 cocktails

½ cup (4 ounces) bourbon
¼ cup (2 ounces) apple cider
¼ cup (2 ounces) fresh lemon juice
2 tablespoons (1 ounce) Simple Syrup (page 156)
2 tablespoons grated fresh ginger
Ice
2 sprigs fresh rosemary, for garnish

THE SUN HOUSE

Charlotte Druckman

Shake some light rum, fresh-squeezed lime juice, and a splash of triple sec with lots of ice, and you have the antidote to a steamy summer day. The author of *Skirt Steak: Women Chefs on Standing the Heat and Staying in the Kitchen* and the cookbook *Stir, Sizzle, Bake,* Charlotte loves this drink because of its backstory. The recipe is based on the signature cocktail of one of her favorite American interior designers, Dick Dumas, who worked with Charlotte's father. Dumas lived abroad, everywhere from France to Southeast Asia, and this particular cocktail is named for his home in Sri Lanka, which is now a boutique hotel.

Makes 2 cocktails

⅓ cup (3 ounces) light rum
2 tablespoons (1 ounce) triple sec
1 tablespoon (½ ounce) Simple Syrup
   (page 156)
⅓ cup (3 ounces) fresh lime juice
Ice

In a cocktail shaker, combine the rum, triple sec, simple syrup, and lime juice. Shake, pour into tall glasses filled with ice, and serve.

COOKIES, CAKES & PIES

WHOLE WHEAT CHOCOLATE CHIP COOKIES
WITH TOASTED WALNUTS

Avery Ruzicka

The secret to these seriously delicious cookies? Toasted walnuts, dark chocolate, and whole wheat flour, which provides a nutty flavor. Avery, the gifted baker behind Manresa Bread in Los Altos and Los Gatos in California, actually mills her own wheat flour and wants you to think beyond the basic chocolate chip cookie we all grew up with. She tinkered with this recipe for some time, trying different ingredients, combinations of flours, and types of sugar until she came up with what is now one of her bakery's most popular items.

Makes 10 cookies

1¾ cups walnuts
¾ cup (1½ sticks) unsalted butter,
   at room temperature
1½ cups packed brown sugar
2 large eggs
1 teaspoon vanilla extract
2⅓ cups whole wheat flour
1 teaspoon kosher salt
¾ teaspoon baking soda
2 cups dark chocolate chunks

Preheat the oven to 350°F.

Spread the walnuts in a single layer on a baking sheet and bake for about 10 minutes. Toss the walnuts after 5 minutes and then every 2 minutes until they are golden brown and start to smell toasted. They burn easily, so keep an eye on them. Remove from the oven, let cool, then coarsely chop and set aside.

In the bowl of a stand mixer fitted with the paddle attachment, cream together the butter and brown sugar on medium speed for about 2 minutes. The mixture should be barely fluffy and almost light brown in color. Be careful not to overmix.

Add the eggs and vanilla and mix for 2 minutes on low speed until combined.

In a separate bowl, whisk together the flour, salt, and baking soda. With the mixer on low speed, add the flour mixture to the bowl with the wet mixture in two increments. Incorporate the chocolate and walnuts on low speed until evenly mixed.

Line two baking sheets with parchment paper. Immediately scoop the cookies with an ice cream scoop onto the prepared baking sheet, leaving plenty of room between the cookies. Gently shape and flatten each cookie until it resembles a hockey puck, about 3 inches wide and at least 1 inch thick.

Refrigerate the prepared cookies for at least 1 hour before baking. This will ensure a soft bake later on.

Preheat the oven to 325°F degrees.

Bake the cookies for about 10 minutes, rotating the baking sheets after 5 minutes, until they are just barely cooked through. Move the baking sheets to wire racks. Let the cookies cool slightly. Enjoy immediately or store in an airtight container. The cookies will keep for several days and get even better a day or so later.

MATCHA & BLACK SESAME FORTUNE COOKIES

Diana Yen

Here are some fortune cookies you'll actually want to eat, courtesy of Diana, the food stylist, recipe tester, and photographer behind the Jewels of New York creative studio. When she moved to the city from the West Coast, Diana started the tradition of making these cookies every Chinese New Year. She prepares the batter ahead and invites friends over for a tea party. They write wishes and fortunes on slips of paper while the cookies bake. It makes for an auspicious start to the year ahead.

Makes about 30 cookies

Nonstick cooking spray
½ cup (1 stick) plus 2 tablespoons unsalted butter
8 large egg whites
1½ cups superfine sugar
2 cups all-purpose flour
¼ teaspoon kosher salt
6 tablespoons heavy cream
2 teaspoons vanilla extract
2 teaspoons matcha powder
2 tablespoons ground black sesame seeds

Print or write fortunes on 2 × ½-inch strips of paper.

Preheat the oven to 375°F. Spray a baking sheet liberally with nonstick cooking spray.

Melt the butter in a small saucepan over low heat and set aside.

In the bowl of a stand mixer fitted with the paddle attachment, beat the egg whites and sugar on medium speed for 30 seconds. Gradually add the flour and salt and beat until incorporated. Add the melted butter, cream, vanilla, and 1 tablespoon water and beat until incorporated.

Divide the batter between two separate bowls. Add the matcha powder to one bowl and the ground black sesame seeds to the other. Stir to combine.

Pour a tablespoon of the matcha batter onto the prepared baking sheet and spread it with the back of a spoon into a thin circle. Repeat with the remaining matcha batter, followed by the black sesame batter. Leave 2 inches of space between each cookie. Bake the cookies on the middle oven rack for 6 to 8 minutes, or until the edges slightly darken. Remove from the oven.

Use an offset spatula to lift up the first cookie, and place a fortune in the center of the cookie. Using your fingers or the end of a wooden spoon, fold the cookie in half and pinch together to form a loose semicircle. Carefully bend the two open ends of the cookie toward each other. Place the cookie in a small bowl or muffin tin and allow it to set for 4 to 5 minutes. Repeat with the remaining cookies. The cookies will keep in an airtight container for up to 1 week.

SPICY GINGER COOKIES

Karlie Kloss

Not all supermodels bake to unwind, but not all supermodels are Karlie Kloss, our very first *Cherry Bombe* cover girl. Karlie became known in fashion circles for bringing baked goods to photo shoots and eventually created her own line of cookies called Klossies. "My gram taught me that baking is a way to show and share love," remembers Karlie. "I learned all my best tricks and techniques from her." This recipe is a version of Gram's gingersnaps; Karlie swapped in some modern ingredients and kept the spiciness for which the wonderfully fragrant treats are known.

Makes 16 cookies

1½ cups oat flour
½ cup almond flour
½ cup coconut sugar
½ teaspoon baking soda
1 teaspoon baking powder
2 teaspoons ground cinnamon
2 teaspoons ground ginger
¼ teaspoon freshly grated nutmeg
¼ teaspoon ground cloves
¼ teaspoon sea salt
6 tablespoons coconut oil, melted
6 tablespoons blackstrap molasses
2 teaspoons vanilla extract

Preheat the oven to 350°F. Line two baking sheets with parchment paper.

In a large bowl, whisk together the oat flour, almond flour, coconut sugar, baking soda, baking powder, cinnamon, ginger, nutmeg, cloves, and salt.

Add the coconut oil, molasses, and vanilla and mix together with your hands or a wooden spoon until a moist ball of dough forms.

Divide the dough into quarters. Divide each quarter into quarters to make 16 pieces total. Roll each piece gently into a ball and place on the prepared baking sheets.

Bake for 8 minutes. Remove from the oven and let cool on a wire rack for 10 to 15 minutes. The cookies will keep for a few days when stored in an airtight container.

VEGAN GLUTEN-FREE CHOCOLATE CHIP COOKIES

Erin McKenna

When this *Cherry Bombe* cover girl opened her first bakery in New York City, her vegan, gluten-free, soy-free, and nut-free chocolate chip cookie made her the queen of the alternative baking scene. "I have eleven brothers and sisters, and we used to bake the same Toll House recipe over and over again, adding twists of our own to achieve the perfect cookie," says Erin, who has since opened Erin McKenna's Bakeries (formerly known as BabyCakes) in Los Angeles and Disney World. "This recipe was so hard won and took months to nail, but when I finally did it, I was walking on air. I think it's one of the best things I've ever done."

Makes about 24 cookies

2 cups Bob's Red Mill gluten-free all-purpose flour (see Tip)

1 cup organic cane sugar or other vegan sugar

¼ cup arrowroot powder

1 teaspoon xanthan gum

1 teaspoon baking soda

1 teaspoon kosher salt

¾ cup unscented coconut oil, melted

6 tablespoons unsweetened applesauce

2 tablespoons vanilla extract

1 cup vegan gluten-free chocolate chips

Preheat the oven to 325°F. Line two baking sheets with parchment paper and set aside.

Combine the flour, sugar, arrowroot, xanthan gum, baking soda, and salt in a medium bowl and whisk until combined. Add the coconut oil, applesauce, and vanilla and stir until smooth. Fold in the chocolate chips.

Drop the dough by the tablespoonful onto the prepared baking sheets, leaving 1 inch between each cookie. Wet your fingers a bit so you can flatten each cookie to about ⅓ inch thick and shape into a neat circle.

Bake for 10 minutes, rotate the pans, and bake for 4 minutes more, or until the cookies are slightly golden. Let cool for 30 minutes. Do not touch the cookies until they are thoroughly cooled or they will break. The cookies will keep for a few days when stored in an airtight container.

Tip: For a cake-like cookie, add an additional 3 tablespoons flour to the amount called for; for a chewier cookie, subtract 2 tablespoons.

YELLOW CAKE
WITH CHOCOLATE FROSTING
Caitlin Freeman

Of course something this delicious comes from Caitlin, the genius pastry chef behind the cookbook *Modern Art Desserts*. (Google her brilliant Mondrian Cake.) This humbler cake is a tribute to Caitlin's single dad, as it re-creates the flavors of the store-bought cake mix and canned frosting he used to make her birthday cakes. Caitlin says the cake can be baked ahead of time, but the frosting should be made right before icing the cake.

Make the cake: Preheat the oven to 350°F. Butter and flour the sides of an 8-inch round cake pan with 3-inch sides and line the bottom with a parchment paper round cut to fit.

In a medium bowl, whisk together the egg yolks, ½ cup of the milk, and the vanilla.

Sift the flour, granulated sugar, baking powder, and salt into the bowl of a stand mixer fitted with the paddle attachment, and mix on low speed for 30 seconds. Add the remaining ¼ cup milk and mix on low speed until moistened, about 15 seconds. Add the butter and beat on medium speed for 1½ minutes, or until smooth and aerated. Scrape down the sides of the bowl with a rubber spatula. Add the egg mixture in three batches, mixing on medium speed for 20 seconds and scraping down the bowl after each addition.

Transfer the batter to the prepared pan and smooth the surface with an offset spatula. Bake for 55 to 60 minutes, rotating the pan midway through baking, until the cake springs back when gently pressed in the center or until a toothpick inserted into the center comes out clean.

Let the cake cool in the pan on a wire rack for 30 minutes, then run an offset spatula around the edges of the pan. Invert the cake onto the wire rack, lift off the pan, and remove the parchment. When the cake is cool enough to handle, after about 20 minutes, flip it again so the top is facing up. Let cool completely, wrap tightly in plastic wrap, and refrigerate for at least 3 hours before assembling.

When the cake is set, make the frosting: In a metal bowl set over a pan of barely simmering water, melt the chocolate, stirring.

Sift the confectioners' sugar, cocoa powder, and salt into the bowl of a stand mixer fitted with the paddle attachment. Add the melted chocolate, milk, and vanilla. Mix on low until all the ingredients are combined. Increase the speed to medium and mix for about a minute more. Using a rubber spatula, scrape down the sides of the bowl, then add the butter. Mix on medium-high speed until the frosting is light and free of lumps.

Frost the cake: Place the cooled cake on a flat, stable work surface. Using a long, serrated knife, slice off the rounded top of the cake so that it is perfectly level. Using the serrated knife, split the cake horizontally into three even layers. Frost the top of each layer, stack the layers, frost the sides of the cake, and serve.

Makes one 3-layer cake

Cake
- ½ cup (1 stick) plus 2 tablespoons unsalted butter, cut into pieces, at room temperature, plus more for the pan
- 2 cups cake flour, plus more for the pan
- 5 large egg yolks, at room temperature
- ¾ cup whole milk, at room temperature
- 1¾ teaspoons vanilla extract
- 1¼ cups granulated sugar
- 1 tablespoon baking powder
- ½ teaspoon kosher salt

Frosting
- 4 ounces unsweetened chocolate, coarsely chopped
- 3½ cups confectioners' sugar
- ⅓ cup unsweetened cocoa powder
- ½ teaspoon kosher salt
- ⅓ cup milk, at room temperature
- 1 teaspoon vanilla extract
- ½ cup (1 stick) unsalted butter, at room temperature

FUNFETTI CAKE
WITH CHERRY FILLING

Molly Yeh

Who doesn't need a little Funfetti in her life? We turned to Molly, arguably the Funfetti Queen of America, to learn how to make a homemade version of this popular cake. The Minnesota-based blogger behind *My Name Is Yeh* has put hours into testing the right kind of sprinkles and the key ingredients for rainbow-studded perfection. For this *Cherry Bombe* version, she adds preserves made with our favorite fruit and tops it with cream cheese frosting. In case you're wondering why Molly uses clear imitation vanilla, it's to keep the cake and the frosting from getting too yellow.

Make the cake: Preheat the oven to 350°F. Grease the bottoms and sides of three 8-inch cake pans and line with parchment paper.

In a medium bowl, whisk together the flour, cornstarch, salt, and baking powder. In the bowl of a stand mixer fitted with the paddle attachment, cream together the butter and granulated sugar until light and fluffy, 3 to 4 minutes. Add the egg whites one at a time, mixing well after each. Add the oil, and vanilla and almond extracts. With the mixer running on low speed, add the dry mixture and the milk in two or three alternating batches and mix until just barely combined. Using a rubber spatula, gently fold in ½ cup of the sprinkles until they're well distributed. Divide the batter evenly among the cake pans.

Bake for about 40 minutes, until a toothpick inserted into the center comes out clean, checking the cake after 25 minutes. Let the layers cool in the pans for 10 minutes and then turn them out onto a wire rack to cool completely.

Make the frosting: In a large bowl using a handheld mixer, beat the cream cheese and butter until smooth. Gradually beat in the confectioners' sugar. Add the salt, vanilla and almond extracts and beat to combine.

Assemble the cake: Place 1 cake layer on a plate. Spread a very thin layer of frosting across the top. Transfer some frosting to a pastry bag fitted with an open star piping tip (alternatively, you can use a zip-top bag and then snip off one corner). Pipe a border of frosting around the top edge of the cake and then spread ½ cup of the cherry preserves over the top of the frosting. (The border will help keep the preserves sealed in.) Place another cake layer on top and repeat the process of frosting, piping on a border, and spreading on cherry preserves. Place the third layer on top and frost the top and sides of the cake with the remaining frosting. Coat the outside of the cake with the remaining sprinkles. The cake will keep at room temperature for up to 2 days and in the refrigerator for up to 1 week.

Makes one 3-layer cake

Cake
1 cup (2 sticks) unsalted butter, at room temperature, plus more for the pans
2½ cups all-purpose flour
¼ cup cornstarch
1 teaspoon kosher salt
2 teaspoons baking powder
1½ cups granulated sugar
4 large egg whites
¼ cup vegetable oil
1 tablespoon clear imitation vanilla extract
½ teaspoon almond extract
¾ cup whole milk
1½ cups artificially colored rainbow sprinkles

Frosting
1 (8 ounce) package cream cheese
6 tablespoons (¾ stick) unsalted butter, at room temperature
2 cups confectioners' sugar
⅛ teaspoon kosher salt
1½ teaspoons clear imitation vanilla extract
¼ teaspoon almond extract

1 cup cherry preserves

ONE-PAN CRAZY CAKE

Amanda Kludt

Meet your new go-to cake recipe. It's a cinch to make, the ingredients are basic and inexpensive, and it's shockingly delicious, given how unfussy it is. You just mix everything in a pie pan and pop it in the oven. The cake comes from Amanda, the editor in chief of *Eater*, the must-read website for the chef- and restaurant-obsessed. Amanda's grandmother made Crazy Cake during World War II as it requires no eggs or butter, so it was one of the few cakes you could make back then when groceries were rationed. Today, Amanda's mom bakes the cake for every family birthday and adds the ultimate girly flourish: pink frosting.

Makes one 9-inch single-layer cake

Cake
1½ cups all-purpose flour
1 cup granulated sugar
1 teaspoon kosher salt
1 teaspoon baking soda
3 tablespoons unsweetened cocoa powder
1 teaspoon vanilla extract
1 tablespoon distilled white vinegar
6 tablespoons vegetable oil
1 cup cold water

Frosting
1 (8-ounce) package cream cheese, at room temperature
1 teaspoon almond extract
1¾ cups confectioners' sugar
Red food coloring or cherry juice

Make the cake: Preheat the oven to 350°F.

Sift the flour, granulated sugar, salt, baking soda, and cocoa powder into a glass pie pan. Gently whisk together, taking care not to let the mixture fly out of the dish.

Make three wells for the liquid ingredients. Pour the vanilla into the first, the vinegar into the second, and the oil into the third. Pour the cold water over the entire mixture and stir until all lumps are gone. If necessary, wipe the batter off the edges of the pan.

Bake for 25 to 30 minutes, or until a toothpick inserted into the center of the cake comes out clean.

Meanwhile, make the frosting: In a medium bowl, mix the cream cheese, almond extract, and confectioners' sugar until well combined. Add a few drops of food coloring and stir until the desired tint is reached.

Once the cake is completely cool, frost the top of it directly in the pan and serve.

BUBBIE SMIGEL CAKE
WITH MOCHA FROSTING

Karen Leibowitz

Reminiscent of babka, this marbled cake is topped with a frosting made of cocoa, confectioners' sugar, and coffee. The recipe is a treasured heirloom for Karen, the San Francisco–based writer and restaurateur behind The Perennial, a sustainable eatery, and the original Mission Chinese Food. Created by her great-grandmother, this old-school dessert is the one most frequently requested by the Leibowitz family. In fact, Karen asked her mother to bake the cake to celebrate the birth of her daughter. "It was the first thing I ate when we came home with our baby."

Make the cake: Preheat the oven to 350°F. Grease a 10-inch Bundt pan.

In the bowl of a stand mixer fitted with the paddle attachment, cream the butter and sugars. One ingredient at a time, mix in the eggs, followed by the flour, sour cream, salt, vanilla, cream of tartar, and baking soda dissolved in water.

In a metal bowl set over a pan of barely simmering water, melt the chocolate, stirring. Using a spatula, fold the chocolate into the batter with just a few strokes—do not stir!—so you end up with a marbled effect.

Pour the batter into the prepared pan and bake for 45 minutes, or until a toothpick inserted into the center comes out clean. Let cool before frosting.

Make the frosting: Combine the butter, coffee, and cocoa in a medium bowl with a wooden spoon. Stir in the salt, then add the confectioners' sugar, ½ cup at a time. Stir well. The frosting should be thick, creamy, and spreadable.

Frost the cake and serve: Turn the cake out onto a plate. Spread the frosting over the outside of the cake. Serve with coffee and birthday candles.

Makes one 10-inch Bundt cake

Cake
1 cup (2 sticks) unsalted butter, at room temperature, plus more for greasing the pan
1 cup packed light brown sugar
1 cup granulated sugar
4 large eggs
2½ cups all-purpose flour
1 cup sour cream
½ teaspoon kosher salt
1 teaspoon vanilla extract
½ teaspoon cream of tartar
1 teaspoon baking soda dissolved in ¼ cup hot water
3 squares unsweetened baking chocolate

Frosting
5 tablespoons unsalted butter, at room temperature
¼ cup brewed coffee, at room temperature
5 tablespoons unsweetened cocoa powder
¼ teaspoon kosher salt
2 cups confectioners' sugar

CHOCOLATE PERSIMMON LOAF CAKE

Amy Guittard

Fans of dark chocolate will be in heaven over this intense loaf, which gets its distinct character from bittersweet Dutch-process cocoa. Persimmon pulp adds moisture and a bit of sweetness. The cake is a riff on a steamed pudding recipe that's been in Amy's family since 1890. Amy, the fifth generation of the San Francisco Guittard Chocolate clan, grew up doing cartwheels in the company's warehouse and climbing over bags of beans. Today, her responsibilities include marketing, sourcing, and sustainability. "This recipe helps me keep a piece of my family history alive," she says. "It's also a great excuse to have chocolate for breakfast."

Makes one 9 × 5-inch loaf

- ½ cup (1 stick) unsalted butter, at room temperature, plus more for the pan
- ½ cup all-purpose flour
- ½ cup whole wheat flour
- 6 tablespoons unsweetened Dutch-process cocoa powder
- 2 teaspoons baking soda
- ½ teaspoon kosher salt
- 1 teaspoon ground cinnamon
- ½ teaspoon ground cloves
- ½ cup granulated sugar
- ½ cup firmly packed light brown sugar
- 2 large eggs
- ½ cup full-fat plain yogurt
- 1½ cups pulp from ripe Hachiya persimmons
- ½ cup dark chocolate baking chips

Preheat the oven to 375°F. Lightly butter a 9-inch square piece of parchment paper, then lay the paper butter-side up inside a 9 x 5-inch loaf pan, leaving the parchment ends hanging over the sides.

In a medium bowl, combine the all-purpose flour, whole wheat flour, cocoa powder, baking soda, salt, cinnamon, and cloves. Set aside.

In a large bowl using a handheld mixer, beat together the butter, granulated sugar, and brown sugar until light and smooth, about 3 minutes. Add the eggs one at a time, then the yogurt, mixing after each addition until smooth. Add the persimmon pulp and the dry mixture in four additions, alternating between the two, mixing after each until well combined. Fold in the baking chips. Pour the batter into the prepared pan.

Bake for 1 hour, or until a toothpick inserted into the center comes out clean. Let the cake cool on a wire rack for 10 minutes. Invert a second wire rack over the top of the cake. Using both hands, flip the cake and rack so the pan is upside down on the rack. Gently shake the pan to release the cake onto the rack. Flip the cake right-side up and allow to cool completely, 2 to 4 hours, before serving. The cake is best the morning after it is made, but it will keep wrapped tightly in plastic at room temperature for up to 5 days, or in the freezer for up to 2 months. To defrost, refrigerate the frozen wrapped cake overnight. Reheat in a 350°F oven for 5 to 10 minutes or until heated through.

Tip: Serve with whipped cream and sliced persimmons or other fresh fruit.

BEST FRIEND CHEESECAKE

Christina Ha

This dessert gets its velvety quality from the addition of whipped egg whites. Christina, the baker, co-owner, and head feline enthusiast behind Manhattan's Macaron Parlour and the Meow Parlour cat café, first made this cheesecake to impress a boyfriend's best friend. (She won them both over; that boyfriend is now her husband and business partner.) One of our favorite facts about our favorite cat lady? She went to a preschool that included cooking and baking as part of the curriculum. Her career path was destined.

Makes one 8-inch cheesecake

Crumb Crust
1 cup graham cracker crumbs
1 tablespoon brown sugar
1½ teaspoons all-purpose flour
¼ teaspoon kosher salt
1½ tablespoons unsalted butter, melted

Cheesecake Filling
2 (8-ounce) packages cream cheese
1 cup plus 1 tablespoon granulated sugar
½ teaspoon vanilla extract
½ vanilla bean, seeds scraped out
½ teaspoon kosher salt
2 large eggs, separated

Sliced strawberries, for serving

Make the crumb crust: Preheat the oven to 325°F. Line an 8-inch round springform pan with parchment paper cut to fit. Coat with nonstick spray. Cover the exterior bottom and sides of the pan with aluminum foil to protect the ingredients while baking in the water bath.

In a large bowl, mix together the graham cracker crumbs, brown sugar, flour, salt, and butter. Press the mixture into the prepared pan to form the crust.

Make the filling: Using a handheld or stand mixer fitted with the paddle attachment, beat together the cream cheese, the 1 cup granulated sugar, the vanilla extract, vanilla bean seeds, and salt. Add the egg yolks and mix until smooth.

Using a handheld mixer, beat the egg whites with the remaining 1 tablespoon sugar until soft peaks form. Gently fold the egg whites into the cream cheese mixture and pour over the crumb crust. Smooth the top of the cheesecake with an offset spatula. Cover the top of the pan with aluminum foil. Put the springform pan in a roasting pan large enough to accommodate it and move both to the oven. Pour hot water into the roasting pan so that it comes 1 inch up the sides of the springform pan.

Bake in the water bath for about 1 hour and 20 minutes, until the center is set and no longer jiggles when you shake the pan. Remove the cake from the pan. Chill for 6 to 8 hours to allow the cheesecake to set completely before serving.

CHOCOLATE HAZELNUT TORTE
WITH WHIPPED CREAM

Elisabeth Prueitt

This refined cake is an ode to classic European tortes, where ground nuts are used instead of white flour. Here, toasted hazelnut flour and rice flour, boosted by coffee and cocoa, achieve a lightness that few gluten-free chocolate cakes can, says Elisabeth, the co-owner and pastry chef behind San Francisco's beloved Tartine bakery and the Manufactory café. She sometimes spreads a thin layer of apricot, raspberry, or strawberry jam under the topping and filling to balance out the chocolate and cream.

Makes one 8-inch layer cake

Cake

¾ cup (1½ sticks) unsalted butter, at room temperature, plus more for greasing the pans

¼ cup white or brown rice flour, plus more for dusting the pans

1 cup plus 2 tablespoons hazelnut flour or finely ground hazelnuts

⅓ cup strong brewed coffee

1 cup granulated sugar

8 ounces bittersweet chocolate, chopped

8 large eggs, separated and at room temperature

½ cup unsweetened Dutch-process cocoa powder, sifted

½ teaspoon sea salt

Filling

1 cup heavy cream

2 tablespoons confectioners' sugar

Make the cake: Preheat the oven to 350°F. Line the bottom of two 8-inch cake pans with parchment paper and butter the paper. Dust the pans with rice flour and tap out any excess.

Toast the hazelnut flour in the oven on a rimmed baking sheet for 2 to 4 minutes, stirring frequently to prevent burning. Set aside to cool.

Combine the coffee and ½ cup of the granulated sugar in a small saucepan over medium heat and stir until the sugar dissolves; remove from the heat. Add the chocolate and stir until the chocolate has melted and is well incorporated. Set aside to cool.

With a handheld mixer on medium-high speed, mix the butter until light and creamy. Reduce the speed to low and add the egg yolks one at a time, beating well after each addition. Using a rubber spatula, fold the chocolate mixture into the butter mixture and set aside.

In a separate bowl, whisk together the rice flour, hazelnut flour, and cocoa powder.

In the bowl of a stand mixer fitted with the whisk attachment, whip the egg whites and salt on medium-high speed until frothy, then gradually add the remaining ½ cup sugar and whip until the mixture holds firm peaks. Sift the flour mixture over the whites and gently fold to incorporate. Mix about one-third of the whites into the chocolate mixture, then fold the chocolate mixture into the rest of the whites.

Divide the batter evenly between the prepared pans. Bake for 30 to 40 minutes, until the tops spring back when lightly touched or a cake tester inserted into the center comes out with a few crumbs clinging to it. Let cool in the pans on a wire rack for 10 minutes. To unmold, run a butter knife around the sides of each pan to loosen. Invert the cakes, lift off the pans, and peel away the parchment. Turn the cakes right side up and let cool completely on the rack.

Make the filling: With a handheld mixer, beat the cream and confectioners' sugar to soft peaks.

Assemble the cake: Transfer the first cake layer to a serving plate. Spread about a third of the whipped cream evenly over the cake layer. Add the second cake layer and spread the remaining whipped cream on the top.

COCONUT CAKE
WITH VANILLA BEAN FROSTING & BERRY FILLING
Amy Chaplin

This naturally sweetened triple-decker cake with creamy coconut frosting is luscious and light. Amy, a private chef and the author of *At Home in the Whole Food Kitchen*, one of the *Cherry Bombe* team's favorite cookbooks, specializes in vegan, whole-grain, and refined sugar–free creations such as this one. "I've served this cake to friends and family on special occasions for years and the look of sheer delight on their faces is always a thrill," she says. "Although I've made many variations, this version is my most requested."

Makes one 8-inch three-layer cake

Frosting
3 (14-ounce) cans coconut milk
½ cup agar flakes
¼ teaspoon sea salt
6 tablespoons grade A maple syrup (see Tip)
¼ cup brown rice syrup
1 vanilla bean
4 teaspoons arrowroot
2 tablespoons filtered water
1 tablespoon vanilla extract

Cake
¾ cup coconut oil, melted, plus more for greasing the pans
3½ cups whole-grain flour
1 tablespoon aluminum-free baking powder
1½ teaspoons baking soda
2½ cups unsweetened, shredded, and full-fat dried coconut
1½ cups grade A maple syrup
1½ cups filtered water
1½ tablespoons raw apple cider vinegar
1 teaspoon sea salt
1 tablespoon vanilla extract

Berry Filling
1 cup fresh or frozen raspberries
1 cup fresh or frozen blueberries
½ cup fresh or frozen blackberries
¾ cup fruit juice–sweetened raspberry jam
1 teaspoon arrowroot
2 teaspoons filtered water

The night before, make the frosting: Combine the coconut milk, agar flakes, salt, maple syrup, and rice syrup in a medium pot. Split the vanilla bean in half lengthwise and scrape the seeds into the pot; add the pod. Bring to a boil over high heat, whisking every minute or so. Reduce the heat to low, cover, and simmer for 15 to 20 minutes, or until the agar flakes have completely dissolved. To check that they have dissolved, remove a small amount of the mixture with a spoon and slowly pour it back into the pot. If you see any translucent pieces of agar, cover the pot and simmer for 5 minutes more before checking again.

Dissolve the arrowroot in the filtered water and slowly pour it into the pan with the coconut milk mixture, whisking continuously. Raise the heat to medium and cook, whisking continuously, until the mixture begins to boil again. Remove from the heat and stir in the vanilla, then pour the mixture into a baking dish or large shallow bowl and let cool. Once the mixture has stopped steaming, remove the vanilla bean pod and refrigerate until cold and solid, about 2 hours.

Cut the frosting into rough 1-inch pieces. They will resemble firm tofu. Transfer them to a food processor and blend until completely smooth. Scrape down the sides as necessary and check for lumps. If the frosting separates, just keep blending until it comes together again—it can take up to 5 minutes to get completely uniform and smooth. Transfer to a container and refrigerate overnight or until completely cool.

Make the cake: Preheat the oven to 350°F. Oil three 8-inch cake pans and line the bottoms of each with parchment paper cut to fit.

Sift the flour, baking powder, and baking soda into a medium bowl. Blend 2 cups of the shredded coconut in a food processor until finely ground. (Be careful not to blend too long, as it will turn into coconut butter.) Add the ground coconut to the flour mixture along with the remaining ½ cup coconut, using a whisk to stir and making sure everything is well combined. Set aside.

In another bowl, whisk the maple syrup, filtered water, oil, vinegar, salt, and vanilla until emulsified. Pour the liquid into the flour mixture and use the whisk to gently stir everything together. Don't overmix. Scrape down the sides of the bowl and check that there are no lumps of flour at the bottom.

(recipe continues)

Tip: Maple syrup "grades" are an indication of color and strength of flavor, not quality.

Divide the mixture evenly among the prepared cake pans. Bake for 20 to 25 minutes, or until the cakes begin to pull away from the edges of the pans and a toothpick inserted into the center comes out clean. The cakes should be a deep golden color.

Remove from the oven and let the cakes cool completely in the pans before turning them out onto individual plates and gently removing the parchment paper.

Make the berry filling: Put the berries and jam in a medium pot and place over medium-high heat. Stir until the mixture begins to simmer, then reduce the heat to low. Cook until the blueberries burst. Dissolve the arrowroot in the filtered water and slowly drizzle it into the pot, stirring continuously. Once the mixture thickens and begins to simmer again, remove from the heat and set aside to cool completely.

Assemble the cake: Be sure that the cake and the berry filling are completely cool and the frosting is well chilled before you begin assembly. Set aside 1 cup of the frosting to decorate the top.

On a flat plate or cake stand, place one cake top-side down. Spread about ½ cup of the frosting over the top, then cover with half of the berry filling. Don't spread the berries all the way to the edges. Repeat with the next layer, then place the third layer on top. Ice the top with frosting. Leave the sides naked; if you prefer, or go ahead and frost them.

Place the reserved frosting in a pastry bag fitted with a metal flower tip. Pipe decorations of your choice around the perimeter of the cake. Place the cake in the refrigerator for at least 30 minutes before serving. As vegan cakes can crumble at room temperature, this cake is best served chilled.

STRAWBERRY RHUBARB PIE

Lisa Donovan

With bright red strawberries, pink rhubarb, and a buttery crust, this sweet-tart pie is so good it just might make you cry. In fact, one night at Margot Café & Bar in Nashville, where Lisa worked as the pastry chef, a guest burst into tears because the pie tasted so much like his grandmother's. Maybe it's all the love that Lisa, a self-taught baker, who also worked at City House and Husk in Nashville, puts into everything she makes. She even skips using a pastry cutter for her pie dough, preferring instead to use her hands for a crust that's truly homemade.

Makes one 10-inch double-crust pie

Crust

2½ cups all-purpose flour, plus more for rolling out the dough
2 teaspoons kosher salt
1 cup plus 6 tablespoons (2¾ sticks) cold unsalted butter, cut into ½-inch pieces

Filling

2 pounds rhubarb, trimmed and cut into ½-inch slices
1½ pounds strawberries, hulled and thickly sliced
¾ cup granulated sugar, plus more for sprinkling
1 vanilla bean
½ cup packed light brown sugar
2 tablespoons cane syrup
Zest and juice of 1 lemon
⅛ teaspoon kosher salt
1 tablespoon all-purpose flour
¼ cup cornstarch

1 large egg

Make the crust: Fill a bowl with 2 cups water and 2 cups ice. Set aside. Toss the flour and salt together in a large bowl. Add the butter cubes and start making smears and butter flakes by working the butter into the flour with your hands. Quickly but gently incorporate all the butter into the flour without overworking it. If the butter feels too warm, place the bowl in the freezer to cool it down. When no whole butter pieces remain, start drizzling ¼ cup of the ice water into the mixture. Use your hands as a paddle to toss the water into the flour until it's fully absorbed. Measure out another ¼ cup of ice water. Drizzle in a bit more and paddle. The dough will begin to form its own ball and not take on any more water. (You will use about ½ cup of ice water, depending on the humidity.) When the dough feels moist, but not wet or sticky, knead it well a few times in the bowl. Divide into two disks and wrap each in plastic. Refrigerate for at least 30 minutes.

Preheat the oven to 425°F.

Roll out the first disk of dough on a lightly floured surface. Move the dough to a 10-inch pie pan and trim the edges to ½ inch outside the rim of the pan. Do not crimp. Refrigerate. Roll out the next disk of dough and lay it flat on a parchment-lined baking sheet. If desired, cut circles, as shown. Refrigerate.

Make the filling: Combine the rhubarb, strawberries, and granulated sugar in a large bowl. Let macerate for 10 to 15 minutes. Drain the juices from the macerated fruit.

Cut the vanilla bean in half and scrape the seeds into the bowl with the fruit; add the brown sugar, cane syrup, lemon zest, lemon juice, and salt and mix together. Whisk the flour and the cornstarch together in a small bowl; stir into the fruit.

Assemble the pie: Whisk the egg with 1 tablespoon water for the egg wash. Mound the filling into the prepared pie pan and brush the rim with the egg wash. Add the top dough, brush with the egg wash, and sprinkle with sugar. If you haven't cut decorations into the top dough, cut three small slits to allow steam to release.

Place the pie on a parchment-paper–lined baking sheet and put in the oven. Reduce the oven temperature to 400°F. Bake for 20 minutes, then reduce the oven temperature once more to 350°F. Bake for 30 to 40 minutes more, until browned and bubbling. Let cool completely on a wire rack, 2 to 3 hours. Serve slightly warm or at room temperature. The pie will keep in the refrigerator for up to 3 days or at room temperature for up to 2 days.

SOUR CHERRY PIE

Emily and Melissa Elsen

Imagine one of the best pies you've ever had, with a filling that bursts with cherry flavor and is mouth-puckering and sweet at the same time—plus a flaky, buttery crust that barely contains the goodness inside. That's the sour cherry pie from Four & Twenty Blackbirds, the Brooklyn-based company founded by sisters Emily and Melissa Elsen. We love this pie so much, it's the first recipe we requested for this book. Adding to the pie's allure is the fact that sour cherry season is so short—it's sometimes as brief as a few weeks. If you see sour cherries where you live, pounce! Buy as many as you can and get baking.

Make the crust: Stir the flour, salt, and granulated sugar together in a large bowl. Add the butter and coat with the flour mixture using a spatula. With a pastry cutter, quickly work the butter into the flour mixture until mostly pea-size pieces remain. (A few larger pieces are okay. Just be careful not to overblend.)

Combine the cold water, vinegar, and ice in a small bowl. Sprinkle 2 tablespoons of the ice water mixture over the flour mixture. Mix and cut it in with a bench scraper or spatula until fully incorporated. Add more of the ice water mixture, 1 to 2 tablespoons at a time, and mix until the dough comes together in a ball, with some dry bits remaining. Squeeze and pinch with your fingertips to bring all the dough together, sprinkling any dry bits with small drops of the ice water mixture, if necessary. Shape the dough into two disks, wrap in plastic, and refrigerate for at least 1 hour or overnight. (Wrapped tightly, the dough can be refrigerated for up to 3 days or frozen for up to 1 month.)

Roll out the first disk of dough on a lightly floured surface and arrange it in a 9-inch pie pan. Refrigerate while you make the filling.

Preheat the oven to 425°F and set racks in the bottom and center positions. Place a rimmed baking sheet on the bottom rack.

Make the filling: Beat the egg in a large bowl. Add the cherries, lemon juice, granulated sugar, brown sugar, arrowroot, allspice, salt, and bitters (if using). Toss well to combine.

Assemble the pie: Roll out the second disk of dough for the top of the pie. Create the design of your choice; or cut slits so steam can escape during baking. Pour the filling into the refrigerated pie shell, arrange the dough on top, and crimp as desired. Refrigerate for 10 to 15 minutes.

Whisk the egg with 1 teaspoon water and the salt. Lightly brush the top of the pie with the egg wash and sprinkle with Demerara sugar. Bake on the rimmed baking sheet on the bottom rack. Bake for 20 to 25 minutes, or until the pastry is set and beginning to brown. Lower the oven temperature to 375°F, move the pie and the baking sheet to the center oven rack, and bake until the pastry is a deep golden brown and the juices are bubbling throughout, 30 to 35 minutes more.

Let the pie cool completely on a wire rack, 2 to 3 hours. Serve slightly warm or at room temperature. The pie will keep in the refrigerator for up to 3 days or at room temperature for up to 2 days.

Makes one 9-inch double-crust pie

Crust
2½ cups unbleached all-purpose flour, plus more for rolling out the dough
1 teaspoon kosher salt
1 tablespoon granulated sugar
1 cup (2 sticks) cold unsalted butter, cut into ½-inch pieces
1 cup cold water
¼ cup apple cider vinegar
1 cup ice

Filling
1 large egg
5 cups sour cherries, pitted
1 tablespoon fresh lemon juice
¾ cup granulated sugar
¼ cup packed light brown sugar
3 tablespoons arrowroot
½ teaspoon ground allspice
½ teaspoon kosher salt
2 dashes Angostura bitters (optional)

1 large egg
Pinch of kosher salt
Demerara sugar, for finishing

DAD'S PERFECT SWEET POTATO PIE

Joy Wilson

This pie is perfection, and comes with a sweet story to boot. Joy, a cookbook author and the talent behind the website *Joy the Baker*, learned how to make this from her father. When she and her sister were little and her dad worked the night shift at the post office, they would bake in the mornings and this was one of his specialties. To this day, Joy prefers sweet potato over pumpkin pie and she loves the untraditional addition of ground coriander, which balances the silky filling.

Makes one 9-inch pie

Crust

1½ cups all-purpose flour, plus more for rolling out the dough
2 teaspoons granulated sugar
½ teaspoon kosher salt
½ cup (1 stick) cold unsalted butter, cut into small cubes
⅓ cup cold buttermilk, plus more as needed

Filling

2 medium sweet potatoes (1½ pounds)
¾ cup packed light brown sugar
1¼ teaspoons ground coriander
½ teaspoon freshly grated nutmeg
½ teaspoon ground cinnamon
¼ teaspoon kosher salt
4 tablespoons (½ stick) unsalted butter
1¼ cups (10 ounces) evaporated milk
⅓ cup granulated sugar
3 large eggs
1 tablespoon vanilla extract

Make the crust: Whisk together the flour, granulated sugar, and salt in a medium bowl. Add the butter and, using your fingers (or a potato masher), quickly work the butter into the flour mixture. Some butter pieces will be the size of oat flakes, some will be the size of peas. Create a well in the mixture and pour in the buttermilk. Use a fork to bring the dough together and moisten all the flour bits. Add a bit more buttermilk, if necessary, to achieve a mixture that's shaggy and not outwardly wet.

On a lightly floured work surface, gently knead the dough into a disk. Wrap in plastic wrap and refrigerate for 1 hour.

On a well-floured surface, roll the chilled dough into a 12-inch disk that is ⅛ inch thick. Carefully transfer the dough to a 9-inch pie pan and trim the outer edges almost even with the edge of the pan. Fold the edges under and crimp with your fingers or a fork. Note that the crust will shrink slightly when baked. Cover with plastic wrap and refrigerate for 30 minutes or up to 3 hours.

Preheat the oven to 375°F. Position a rack in the upper third of the oven.

Make the filling: Peel the sweet potatoes and cut into 3-inch chunks. Put the pieces in a large pot and cover with cool water. Bring the water to a boil over medium-high heat. Reduce the heat to medium and simmer until the potatoes are tender throughout, 15 to 20 minutes. Drain in a colander.

Return the potatoes to the pot and add the brown sugar, coriander, nutmeg, cinnamon, salt, butter, and about half of the evaporated milk. Use a potato masher to break down the potatoes and cook over low heat for 5 minutes. Use an immersion blender or a food processor to get the mixture as smooth as possible. Let cool.

In a medium bowl, whisk together the remaining evaporated milk, the granulated sugar, eggs, and vanilla. Whisk well. Pour into the warm sweet potato mixture and combine. The filling will be liquidy at this point.

Pour the filling into the pie crust. Bake the pie on a baking sheet for 10 minutes. Reduce the oven temperature to 325°F and bake until cooked through, 45 to 50 minutes. To test the pie for doneness, lightly shake the baking sheet. If the center of the pie has a "wavy jiggle," as Joy describes it, keep the pie in the oven. If the center of the pie has a lighter, more structured jiggle, it's done. Let the pie cool, then refrigerate. It's best served chilled.

CROSTATA DELLA NONNA

Gabriela Cámara

As the talent behind San Francisco's Cala restaurant, Gabriela is celebrated for her Mexican cuisine, but one of her most-loved recipes comes from the Italian side of her family. This *crostata*—a dessert somewhere between a pie, a tart, and a galette—originated with her maternal great-grandmother, Nonna Clara, who lived in Tuscany. Gabriela learned how to make it from her grandmother, Nonna Anna. You can put your own spin on the *crostata* by substituting your favorite flavor of jam and adjusting the amount of sugar in the dough.

Makes two 9-inch round crostatas

5 cups all-purpose flour, plus
  more for rolling out the dough
1½ cups granulated sugar
5 teaspoons baking powder
⅛ teaspoon kosher salt
1 cup (2 sticks) cold unsalted
  butter, cut into ½-inch cubes,
  plus more for greasing the pans
5 large eggs
Zest of 1 lemon
¼ cup vin santo or other sweet wine
1½ cups apricot, raspberry,
  or strawberry jam

In a large bowl, whisk together the flour, sugar, baking powder, and salt. With your fingertips or a pastry blender, work in the butter until most of the mixture resembles coarse meal with pea-size lumps.

In a small bowl, whisk together 4 of the eggs, the lemon zest, and wine until well combined. Stir into the flour mixture. Gently knead the mixture just until it forms a dough. Divide evenly into 3 balls and form into flattened disks. Wrap in plastic wrap and refrigerate for 2 hours or up to overnight.

Preheat the oven to 375°F. Butter two 9-inch tart pans.

On a lightly floured surface, roll the first disk of dough into a circle about ¼ inch thick and 1 inch larger than your tart pan. Press the dough into the bottom and sides of the pan. Trim any overhang with a knife. Repeat with the second disk of dough in a second tart pan. Spread ¾ cup of jam evenly in the bottom of each.

In a small bowl, beat the remaining egg with 1 tablespoon water. Set aside. To make the lattice tops, roll the remaining disk of dough into a circle about to ¼ inch thick. Cut the circle of dough into ½-inch-wide strips, long enough to cover the pan. Place the strips horizontally, evenly spaced across the top of one pan. Then lay the strips perpendicularly on top of the horizontal strips. Crimp the edges of the dough with a fork to seal and trim off any excess. Repeat with the second pan. Brush the top of the dough with the beaten egg. Bake for 20 to 25 minutes, until the crust is golden brown. Serve warm or at room temperature.

CHERRY BOMBE CAKE BALLS

Justine D.

These epic "cherries" are the most decadent cake balls around: They're blended with homemade buttercream frosting, dipped in bittersweet chocolate, tickled with edible red luster, and finished with a glassy green candy stem. They don't need a cherry on top—they *are* the cherry on top. These mini masterpieces were created by Justine D., who is both a popular New York DJ and a classically trained pastry chef. To channel Justine's rock-and-roll spirit, roll up your sleeves, turn up your playlist, and get ready for a good time in your kitchen. You're the bombe, and so are these cake balls.

Makes about 24 cake balls

Chocolate Cake
4 tablespoons (½ stick) unsalted butter, melted and cooled, plus more for the pan
1 cup all-purpose flour, plus more for the pan
1 cup granulated sugar
⅔ cup sifted Dutch-process cocoa powder
¾ teaspoon baking powder
¾ teaspoon baking soda
½ teaspoon kosher salt
1 large egg, at room temperature
½ cup buttermilk, at room temperature
1½ teaspoons vanilla extract
½ cup strong brewed hot coffee

Swiss Meringue Buttercream
⅓ cup sugar
3 tablespoons egg whites
½ cup (1 stick) cold unsalted butter, cut into cubes
½ teaspoon vanilla extract
⅛ teaspoon kosher salt

24 ounces bittersweet baking chocolate
2 cups sugar
¾ cup light corn syrup
Green food coloring
Edible red pearlescent luster dust

Make the cake: Preheat the oven to 350°F. Butter and flour an 8-inch cake pan.

In the bowl of a stand mixer fitted with the paddle attachment, combine the sugar, flour, cocoa powder, baking powder, baking soda, and salt and mix on low speed until well combined. Slowly add the egg, buttermilk, butter, and vanilla, then increase the speed to medium and beat for 2 minutes. Slowly beat in the hot coffee.

Pour the batter into the prepared pan and bake on the middle rack of the oven for 35 to 40 minutes, rotating halfway through baking, until a toothpick inserted into the center comes out clean. Let cool completely on a wire rack.

Meanwhile, make the buttercream: Whisk together the sugar and egg whites in the bowl of a stand mixer. Place the bowl over a pan of simmering water (do not let the water touch the bottom of the bowl) and cook, whisking continuously, until the sugar has dissolved and the temperature of the mixture registers 140°F on a candy thermometer.

Return the bowl to the mixer and use the whisk attachment to beat the mixture on medium speed, gradually increasing to medium-high, until stiff peaks form. Once the meringue has completely cooled, begin to add the butter, several tablespoons at a time. Add the vanilla and salt, then switch to the paddle attachment and beat on medium-high speed for 2 minutes until smooth.

To make the Cherry Bombes, in a large bowl, crumble the cooled cake with your hands until there are no large pieces left. Using a large spoon, add the buttercream and mix well. With your hands, roll the cake mixture into 1½-inch balls. Place the balls on a baking sheet lined with wax paper, cover with plastic wrap, and refrigerate for 2 to 3 hours, until firm.

Once the cake balls are chilled, chop the bittersweet chocolate into chunks, reserving a 1-inch "seed" piece for tempering. (Tempering is a technique that ensures the chocolate coating will be glossy and crisp.) Put the chocolate in a heatproof bowl set over a pan of simmering water (do not let the bottom of the bowl touch the water). Heat the chocolate, stirring if necessary, until it has melted and registers 115 to 120°F on a candy thermometer. Remove from the heat and drop the reserved 1-inch piece of chocolate into the bowl. Stir frequently and let the chocolate cool to 80 to 85°F.

(recipe continues)

Place the chocolate back over the pan of simmering water and return the temperature to 88 to 91°F. Remove any remaining bit of the "seed" chocolate. The chocolate is now ready for dipping. If the temperature drops, rewarm it gently.

Insert a wooden skewer into the center of a cold cake ball and dip the ball into the tempered chocolate. Shake off any excess chocolate, return to baking sheet, and remove the skewer. Repeat with the remaining cake balls.

Line a separate baking sheet with wax paper. Place a Silpat liner on a third baking sheet.

In a large saucepan, combine the sugar, corn syrup, and ½ cup water. Bring to a boil over medium heat, stirring occasionally. Cover and cook for 3 minutes to dissolve the sugar crystals. Uncover and cook over medium-high heat, without stirring, until a candy thermometer registers 300°F. Remove from the heat and stir in the green food coloring.

Place a double layer of latex gloves on your hands. Working quickly, pour half the melted sugar onto the Silpat and let cool until you can work it with your hands. The sugar should still be warm and easy to manipulate, with a texture similar to saltwater taffy.

To make leaves, pull a small amount of sugar and form it into little cherry leaves with your thumb and index fingers pressed together. Place the finished leaves on the baking sheet lined with wax paper. The leaves should all look different. If the sugar hardens, place it back in the saucepan over low heat and melt again, repeating this process as many times as necessary.

To make stems, dip a spoon into the melted sugar and drip in thin 2-inch lines over the Silpat. Use some melted sugar to adhere the leaves to each stem. Place on the wax paper–lined baking sheet to harden. Rewarm the reserved sugar if necessary.

Using a paintbrush, dab the luster dust onto the chocolate-covered cake balls. Carefully place a stem into each cake ball through the skewered hole in the top. Serve at room temperature.

SWEET TREATS

CANDIED GRAPEFRUIT POPS

Amanda Cohen

It's a revelation to bite into these unique lollipops, half fresh fruit, half crunchy candy shell. The inspiration? Beijing street food. "Several years ago, I took a two-day train trip to the city and was starving when I got there," says Amanda, the inventive New York City chef. "The city was cold and gray and I saw this guy selling candied orange slices on a stick. These juicy, sweet things lit up the entire street." Amanda swapped in grapefruit for a bolder contrast of flavors and served the pops as part of the very first menu at her vegetarian restaurant Dirt Candy.

Makes 10 lollipops

10 grapefruit segments
3 cups granulated sugar

Place a piece of floral foam or heavy Styrofoam on a serving platter to hold the skewers upright. Set aside.

Push a bamboo skewer lengthwise through each grapefruit segment.

Pour the sugar and 3 cups water into a heavy-bottomed pot. Heat the mixture, without stirring, over medium-high heat until it turns light brown and registers 275 to 300°F on a candy thermometer, about 20 minutes. Do not stir.

Dip each skewered grapefruit piece into the hot syrup and coat thoroughly, being very careful with the hot sugar.

Stick the skewer into the piece of foam and let dry upright until a hard shell forms. Repeat with the remaining segments.

BROKEN PIE CRUST COBBLER
WITH MIXED BERRIES

Cassidee Dabney

This deconstructed take on Southern cobbler features flaky pie crust pieces layered with a raspberry, blueberry, and blackberry filling and baked until bubbling. For Cassidee, the executive chef at Blackberry Farm, the Tennessee resort with a celebrated culinary program, this sweet celebration of summer brings back childhood memories of picking wild blackberries in her grandma's cow pasture in rural Arkansas and long weekend trips to Pine Mountain in Southwest Virginia to pick wild high-bush blueberries.

Makes 8 servings

Crust

1¼ cups all-purpose flour, plus more
    for rolling out the dough
½ teaspoon kosher salt
10 tablespoons (1¼ sticks) cold
    unsalted butter, plus more
    to grease the baking dish
2 to 3 tablespoons ice water,
    as needed

Filling

½ cup granulated sugar
¼ cup cornstarch
6 cups fresh or frozen mixed berries
    (Cassidee prefers raspberries,
    blueberries, and blackberries)
2 tablespoons fresh lemon juice

2 tablespoons granulated sugar
½ teaspoon ground cinnamon
Vanilla ice cream, for serving

Make the crust: In a large bowl, combine the flour and the salt. Using a box grater, grate the butter into the flour mixture. Working quickly with your hands, pinch the butter into the flour until it resembles coarse crumbs. Stir in the ice water, 1 tablespoon at a time, until the mixture forms a ball. Wrap in plastic and refrigerate for 2 hours.

Preheat the oven to 350°F and set a rack in the middle position. Line two baking sheets with parchment paper.

Make the filling: Mix together the sugar and cornstarch in a large pot. Add the berries and lemon juice and toss until evenly coated. Cook over medium heat until the mixture begins to bubble. Simmer, stirring continuously, for 3 to 5 minutes (7 to 10 minutes for frozen berries), until slightly thickened. Set aside.

Assemble the cobbler: In a small bowl, combine the sugar and cinnamon. Divide the dough into two sections. On a lightly floured surface, roll each section into a ⅛-inch-thick sheet. Place the dough on the baking sheets and sprinkle with the cinnamon-sugar mixture. Bake until the pie crust begins to turn golden, 25 to 30 minutes. Remove from the oven and let cool; keep the oven on.

Grease an 8-inch square baking dish with butter. Spoon half the berry mixture into the baking dish. Crack the cooked piecrust into large pieces and cover the berry mixture with a layer of the crust, reserving some for the top. Spoon the remaining berry mixture on top. Finish with more pieces of the piecrust.

Bake for 10 to 15 minutes, until the crust begins to brown. Let the cobbler cool to room temperature. Serve with vanilla ice cream.

PORTOKALOPITA
(GREEK BREAD PUDDING WITH PHYLLO & YOGURT)

Mina Stone

This intriguing take on bread pudding has syrup dripping from every forkful and is fragrant with cinnamon and orange. We're talking about *portokalopita*, a dessert that uses phyllo dough as its main ingredient. Mina, the private chef who charmed the food and art worlds with her book *Cooking for Artists*, discovered this dish on vacation in Karpenisi, a small mountain village in Greece. While there, she enjoyed one of the best meals of her life, thanks to a woman named Evgenia. "She had a small restaurant, with bright lighting, dancing elves painted on the walls, and a weird atmosphere," recalls Mina. "When I asked about the dessert, she didn't bat an eye but instead generously wrote down her recipe to share with me. I have been making it ever since."

Makes 8 to 10 servings

Bread Pudding

1 cup safflower or other neutral oil, plus more for greasing the pan
4 large eggs
7 ounces plain 2% Greek yogurt
½ cup granulated sugar
Zest of 1 orange
2½ teaspoons baking powder
1 (16-ounce) package phyllo dough

Syrup

2 cups granulated sugar
1 cinnamon stick
2 strips orange peel
¼ teaspoon sea salt

Make the bread pudding: Preheat the oven to 350°F. Lightly oil a 10-inch round cake pan.

In a large bowl, whisk together the eggs and safflower oil until emulsified. Add the yogurt, sugar, orange zest, and baking powder and whisk to combine.

Tear each phyllo sheet into pieces roughly the size of your hand. Add the phyllo in batches to the yogurt mixture and fold them in gently, making sure there are no dry spots.

Pour the phyllo mixture into the prepared pan and bake until golden brown, 45 to 55 minutes.

Meanwhile, make the syrup: Combine the sugar, cinnamon stick, orange peel, salt, and 2 cups water in a medium saucepan and bring to a boil. Reduce to medium-low heat and simmer until the mixture thickens, about 10 minutes. Remove from the heat and let the syrup cool.

Finish the bread pudding: Remove the pan from the oven, poke holes in the cake with a wooden dowel or a chopstick, and slowly pour the cooled syrup over the hot cake. (It will seem like a lot of syrup, but don't worry.)

Let the cake sit for at least 30 minutes before serving. It's best served slightly warm, but it's delicious at room temperature, too. Store covered in the refrigerator for up to 3 days.

COCONUT BANANA BREAD
WITH GINGER & FLAXSEEDS

Camille Becerra

Team *Cherry Bombe* fell in love with this treat when Camille was working at Cafe Henrie in Manhattan, just a few blocks from our old office. We'd visit almost daily to buy a slice of the sexiest banana bread you could ever dream of. For her recipe, Camille, now the chef at De Maria in New York, took basic banana bread and updated it with coconut, yogurt, and crystallized ginger. The outside of the loaf is coated with flaxseeds, which lend a toasty crunch.

Makes one 9 × 5-inch loaf

- ½ cup coconut oil, melted, plus more for greasing the pan
- ⅓ cup flaxseeds
- 4 bananas: 3 mashed, 1 cut in half lengthwise
- ½ cup organic cane sugar
- 2 large eggs
- ½ cup plain yogurt
- 1½ cups all-purpose flour
- 1 teaspoon kosher salt
- 1 teaspoon baking soda
- ½ cup unsweetened shredded coconut
- ¼ cup chopped crystallized ginger

Preheat the oven to 375°F. Grease a 9 × 5-inch loaf pan with coconut oil and coat the inside with the flaxseeds.

Mix the mashed bananas, coconut oil, sugar, eggs, and yogurt together in a large bowl.

In another bowl, combine the flour, salt, baking soda, coconut, and ginger. Add the dry ingredients to the wet ingredients and stir well to incorporate.

Spoon the batter into the prepared pan and bake for 15 minutes. Remove the pan from the oven and garnish with the halved banana on top. Reduce the oven temperature to 350°F and bake for 40 to 50 minutes more, or until a cake tester inserted into the center of the loaf comes out clean.

Let cool in the pan for 15 minutes before removing it to a cutting board and slicing. Enjoy for breakfast or with late-afternoon coffee or tea. The loaf will keep at room temperature, wrapped in plastic wrap, for up to 3 days.

Tip: If you see brown or blackened bananas at the grocery store, snap them up. They're perfect for making banana bread.

LEMON POPPY SEED MUFFINS

Christina Tosi

Lemon lovers, rejoice! These muffins have juice, zest, and bursty bits of the sunny citrus baked right in. Christina, the brains behind the Milk Bar shops and its now-iconic Cereal Milk, Crack Pie, and Compost Cookies, created these treats in tribute to her number one hero and role model—her mother. "She will do anything for lemon poppy seed," said the *Cherry Bombe* cover girl and *MasterChef* judge. "As such, I was inspired to create a recipe for the remarkable woman I get to call Mom!"

Makes 24 muffins

Batter
8 lemons
5 large egg whites
¾ cup (1½ sticks) unsalted butter
1¾ cups granulated sugar
⅓ cup packed light brown sugar
5 large egg yolks
¾ cup crème fraîche or sour cream
2⅔ cups all-purpose flour
2 tablespoons poppy seeds
1 teaspoon kosher salt
1 teaspoon baking powder
½ teaspoon baking soda

Glaze
Juice of 2 lemons
2 cups confectioners' sugar

Preheat the oven to 350°F. Line two 12-cup muffin tins with paper liners.

Make the batter: Zest the lemons, then cut off the top and bottom of each zested lemon. With each lemon upright, resting on its newly flat bottom, cut off the white pith in a curved slicing motion until only the fruit is left. Run a paring knife along each segment to release and remove it from the membrane, being sure to remove all the seeds as well. Cut the segments lengthwise into little slivers. Combine the lemon segments, any remaining juice, and the zest in a bowl and set aside.

In the bowl of a stand mixer fitted with the whisk attachment, whip the egg whites on high speed until they hold medium-firm peaks. Transfer them to another bowl and set aside. Clean and dry the stand mixer bowl.

In the bowl of the stand mixer fitted with the paddle attachment, cream the butter and sugars on medium-high speed until light and fluffy, about 3 minutes. Reduce the speed to low, then add the egg yolks and crème fraîche. Mix until well combined, about 1 minute.

In a separate bowl, whisk together the flour, poppy seeds, salt, baking powder, and baking soda. With the stand mixer on low speed, add the flour mixture and the lemon juice, zest, and segments to the wet mixture in intervals, alternating between the lemon and the flour.

Add ½ cup of the whipped egg whites to the batter and mix on low until well combined, about 1 minute. Turn off the mixer and fold the remaining egg whites into the batter with a rubber spatula until well combined, being careful not to deflate the egg whites too much.

Pour the batter into the muffin tins, making sure each well is no more than three-quarters full. Bake for 20 minutes, or until a toothpick inserted into the center of one of the muffins comes out clean.

Place the individual muffins on a wire rack to cool.

Make the glaze: Put the lemon juice in a medium bowl. Gently whisk in the confectioners' sugar until a thick, smooth glaze forms. Drizzle a bit of glaze over each muffin and serve.

IRISH SODA BREAD

Alissa Wagner

You don't have to be Irish to love this bread. Take a warm slice, spread on a little butter, sprinkle with some flaky sea salt, and we promise that this dense, slightly sweet bread will become your new favorite. Or try it Alissa's way—plain with a cup of steaming PG Tips tea. This might not be the first recipe you'd expect from the chef of Dimes NYC, the influential restaurant known for its healthy, seasonal, and photogenic food. But this recipe was passed from Alissa's grandmother to her aunt, who always made it for Alissa when she was growing up.

Makes one 9 × 5-inch loaf

1¼ tablespoons unsalted butter,
   plus more for greasing the pan
2½ cups all-purpose flour
½ cup granulated sugar
½ teaspoon kosher salt
1 teaspoon baking powder
⅛ teaspoon baking soda
⅛ teaspoon cream of tartar
1 large egg
1 cup whole milk
¾ cup raisins

Preheat the oven to 375°F. Grease a 9 × 5-inch loaf pan with butter.

Melt the butter in a small saucepan and set aside.

Sift the flour, sugar, salt, baking powder, baking soda, and cream of tartar into a medium bowl.

In another medium bowl, beat the egg until fluffy, then add the milk and beat for 2 minutes more. Add the melted butter and the egg mixture to the flour mixture and mix until thoroughly combined. Stir in the raisins.

Transfer the dough into the loaf pan. Poke any visible raisins under the surface so they don't burn. Bake for 45 minutes, or until golden brown and a toothpick inserted into the middle comes out clean.

Tip: Alissa says this traditional dough base lends itself to different combinations of dried fruits and spices. You can swap out the raisins for chopped dried figs, dried apricots, or dried sour cherries and mix a teaspoon of ground cardamom, cinnamon, or nutmeg into the dry ingredients.

BUÑUELOS PELANCHON
(MEXICAN FRITTERS)

Bertha González Nieves

Buñuelos are often made during the holidays, when family and friends are around to celebrate. Good times and Mexican heritage are important to Bertha, who cofounded the small-batch tequila company Casa Dragones and who inherited this recipe from her great-grandmother. Here, these crispy delights are drizzled with an anise-and-orange–scented syrup sweetened with *piloncillo*, an unrefined sugar made from cane juice. Imagine brown sugar with a flavor that brings to mind rum, smoke, and molasses.

Make the dough: In the bowl of a stand mixer fitted with the dough hook, combine the flour, baking powder, sugar, and salt. With the mixer on low speed, add the eggs, then the vegetable shortening, followed by ¾ cup water.

Increase the speed to medium and mix for 2 to 3 minutes, or until the dough is stiff and pulls away from the sides of the bowl. When you press the dough with your fingertip, it should leave an imprint.

Cover the dough with a towel and let rest for about 30 minutes. With floured palms, roll the dough into Ping-Pong-size balls. With a rolling pin, flatten each ball until it forms a circle 4 to 5 inches in diameter.

Make the syrup: Combine the *piloncillo*, star anise, orange peel, and ½ cup water in a small saucepan and bring to a boil. Reduce the heat to medium-low and simmer for 5 to 10 minutes, or until the liquid has reduced by about a third. Remove the orange peel and star anise. Keep warm.

Cook the *buñuelos*: Preheat the oven to the lowest temperature. Line a baking sheet or metal rack with paper towels.

Heat ¾ inch of oil in a large heavy skillet over medium-high heat until the oil bubbles when a wooden skewer is inserted into the center. Add the *buñuelos* one or two at a time and fry for 30 seconds on each side, or until brown and crispy.

Transfer the *buñuelos* to the prepared baking sheet as you finish them, layering more paper towels as necessary to absorb the excess oil. Keep the baking sheet in the oven set to the lowest temperature.

To serve, place the *buñuelos* on a plate and drizzle with the warm syrup.

Makes 30 buñuelos

Dough

3⅓ cups all-purpose flour, plus more for rolling out the dough
½ tablespoon baking powder
1½ tablespoons granulated sugar
½ teaspoon kosher salt
2 large eggs, beaten and at room temperature
6 tablespoons vegetable shortening

Syrup

1 (4-ounce) *piloncillo* cone, or 1 cup packed dark brown sugar
1 star anise pod
Peel of ¼ orange, pith removed

3 cups vegetable oil, for frying

HONEY SEMIFREDDO

Elise Kornack

If you've never cooked with honey before, you're in for a treat, as its fragrance and complexity are really eye opening. Elise, who was the chef behind Take Root, the Brooklyn jewel box of a restaurant she ran with her wife, Anna Hieronimus, loves nothing more than transforming familiar ingredients. She refers to it as walking that fine line between "comfort and intrigue." Semi-freddo, a traditional Italian dessert, is an impressive final course and a great alternative to ice cream—especially if you want to make something homemade and don't have an ice cream maker.

Makes 4 servings

¼ teaspoon unflavored powdered gelatin
¾ cup heavy cream
3 tablespoons honey
2 tablespoons granulated sugar
⅛ teaspoon kosher salt
3 large egg yolks
1 teaspoon vanilla extract
Seasonal fruit, for serving

Combine the gelatin with 1 tablespoon water in a small bowl or cup. Set aside.

In the bowl of a stand mixer fitted with the whisk attachment or using a handheld mixer, whip the cream on medium to medium-high speed until it holds soft peaks. Refrigerate.

Combine the honey, sugar, salt, and 2 tablespoons water in a small saucepan. Bring to a boil over medium heat, stirring occasionally to dissolve everything. Stop stirring and let the mixture boil for 3 to 5 minutes, until a candy thermometer registers 238°F. Tilt the pan if necessary to get the reading, but be careful not to splash the hot liquid.

In the bowl of a stand mixer fitted with the whisk attachment or using a handheld mixer, beat the yolks on high speed until they are thick and light yellow in color. Reduce the speed to low and slowly add the honey mixture, avoiding the whisk and the sides of the bowl. (Do not clean the hot honey pan.)

Add the gelatin mixture to the hot honey pan and swirl to dissolve. Add the gelatin-honey mixture along with the vanilla to the egg mixture and beat for 3 to 5 minutes, until it has cooled and thickened.

Using a rubber spatula, fold one-third of the whipped cream into the mixture until combined, then gently mix in the remaining whipped cream. Divide the mixture among four ramekins and cover with plastic wrap. Freeze for several hours. Serve topped with seasonal fruit.

MAPLE CHOCOLATE PUDDING
WITH BACON SPOONS

Katrina Markoff

This pudding is one of the glossiest, richest, and, yes, chocolatiest you will ever taste. And did we mention that your "spoon" is actually a crisp piece of candied bacon, fragrant with smoked paprika? Genius flavor pairings such as this one have become a signature for Katrina and the two companies she founded, Vosges Haut-Chocolat and Wild Ophelia Chocolates. For this dessert, she took inspiration from her favorite childhood breakfast of chocolate chip pancakes, bacon, and Aunt Jemima syrup.

Makes 8 servings

8 thick-cut bacon slices

2 tablespoons turbinado sugar

2 teaspoons smoked paprika

10 ounces milk chocolate (in the range of 45% cacao)

2 vanilla beans

1½ cups heavy cream

⅔ cup grade B maple syrup (see Tip, page 192)

1 teaspoon smoked sea salt (such as Alderwood)

Preheat the oven to 375°F. Line a baking sheet with parchment paper.

Arrange the bacon slices on the prepared baking sheet and sprinkle with the turbinado sugar and paprika. Bake for 30 minutes, or until firm and crispy. Set aside.

In a metal bowl set over a pan of simmering water, melt the chocolate, stirring regularly.

Split the vanilla beans lengthwise and scrape the seeds into a medium saucepan. Add the pods, the cream, and maple syrup and bring to a boil over medium heat. Turn off the heat and let the cream infuse and cool for 10 minutes.

Pour the melted chocolate into a blender or food processor. Remove the vanilla bean pods from the cream and pour the cream-vanilla infusion over the chocolate. Blend together until a glossy emulsion has formed.

Fill eight low glasses with the warm pudding and let set for 10 minutes to thicken slightly. Sprinkle each pudding with a pinch of smoked salt and stand a piece of bacon in the center. Encourage guests to use the bacon as a "spoon."

RIZ AU LAIT
(FRENCH RICE PUDDING)

Christine Muhlke

A devoted Francophile, Christine fell in love with the *riz au lait* at the Paris bistro L'Ami Jean, where it's presented family-style with an array of home-made toppings. The editor and cookbook author now makes it for friends in need of something sweet and comforting. The rice pudding itself is toothsome but cloud-like, thanks to the whipped cream folded in right before serving. This recipe first appeared in the *New York Times Magazine*, where Christine wrote the influential "Field Report" column about farmers and food artisans for several years. Thank you to the *Times* food team for letting us share this.

Makes 6 to 8 servings

Confiture de Lait
1 (14-ounce) can sweetened condensed milk
½ teaspoon sea salt

Crème Anglaise
½ vanilla bean
1 cup heavy cream
⅓ cup whole milk
6 tablespoons granulated sugar
3 large egg yolks

Brittle
⅔ cup unsalted blanched hazelnuts or pistachios
Unsalted butter, for greasing the pan
1 dried apricot, finely chopped
½ teaspoon kosher salt
⅔ cup granulated sugar

Riz au Lait
½ vanilla bean
2 cups plus 2 tablespoons whole milk
½ cup carnaroli, Arborio, or short-grain rice
2½ tablespoons granulated sugar
1⅔ cups heavy cream

Make the *confiture de lait*: Preheat the oven to 425°F.

Bring a kettle of water to a boil. Pour the condensed milk into a glass pie pan or shallow baking dish. Stir in the sea salt and cover tightly with aluminum foil. Set the pan in a separate larger pan. Pour hot water from the kettle into the larger pan until the water comes halfway up the sides of the pie pan. Bake until the milk turns caramel-brown, 1 to 1¼ hours. Check the water level several times and add more as needed.

Let cool in the larger pan. Whisk if lumpy. Keep the *confiture de lait* refrigerated until ready to serve, then warm gently in a hot-water bath.

Make the crème anglaise: Split the vanilla bean, scrape out the seeds, and place the bean and seeds in a small pot. Add the cream, milk, and 3 tablespoons of the sugar and heat over medium heat until almost boiling. Remove from the heat.

Meanwhile, in a medium bowl, whisk the egg yolks and the remaining 3 table-spoons sugar until fluffy. Whisk just enough of the scalded cream mixture into the egg yolks to warm them, then pour the yolks into the cream mixture.

Stir with a wooden spoon in a figure-eight motion over low heat until the mixture coats the back of the spoon and the bubbles along the edge disappear. Pass the mixture through a fine-mesh sieve into a bowl set over an ice bath. Let cool completely, then refrigerate.

Make the brittle: Preheat the oven to 350°F. Place the hazelnuts on a rimmed baking sheet. Toast in the oven for 10 to 15 minutes, stirring every few minutes, until they smell fragrant and toasty. Let cool, then coarsely chop.

Butter a baking sheet. In a small bowl, mix the hazelnuts, apricot, and kosher salt. Cook the sugar in a medium pot over high heat, without stirring. As it starts to turn deep caramel, swirl the pan to distribute the sugar. Once the sugar has dissolved, remove from the heat and fold in the hazelnuts and apricot. Pour the liquid onto the prepared baking sheet and let cool. Break into small pieces.

(recipe continues)

Make the *riz au lait*: Split the vanilla bean, scrape out the seeds, and place the bean and seeds in a medium saucepan. Add the milk and bring to a simmer. Stir in the rice and simmer, stirring occasionally, until it reaches the consistency of oatmeal, 25 to 30 minutes. Stir in the sugar. Let cool to room temperature, then refrigerate.

Transfer the chilled rice to a large bowl and remove the vanilla bean pod.

In another bowl, whip the cream to stiff peaks with a handheld mixer. Fold the whipped cream into the rice, little by little, to the desired thickness. It should be light and creamy.

Serve the *confiture de lait, crème anglaise,* and brittle in separate bowls alongside the *riz au lait,* to be stirred in as desired.

SALTED CARAMEL BROWNIES

Agatha Kulaga and Erin Patinkin

This luscious baked good was born when a friend asked Agatha and Erin to create a "kick-ass brownie" as a special for his restaurant. "We decided to top some brownie batter with our salted caramel sauce, and voilà!" recalls Agatha. The result was these "magical and indulgent" brownies. After meeting at a food-focused book club, Agatha and Erin founded the popular Brooklyn bakery Ovenly in 2010. It has since evolved into a multilocation and wholesale operation with a mission to be socially responsible.

Makes 16 brownies

Brownies

½ cup (1 stick) plus 2 tablespoons unsalted butter, cubed, plus more for greasing the pan

⅔ cup all-purpose flour, plus more for dusting the pan

1 cup chopped dark chocolate (60 to 65% cacao)

1 cup granulated sugar

⅓ cup packed light brown sugar

3 large eggs, at room temperature

1 teaspoon vanilla extract

3 tablespoons unprocessed cocoa powder

¼ teaspoon kosher salt

Salted Caramel Sauce (recipe follows)

Make the brownies: Preheat the oven to 350°F. Grease an 8-inch square baking pan with butter and dust it with flour.

Place the chocolate and butter in a medium heatproof bowl. Place the bowl over a saucepan filled with 1 inch of cold water to create a double boiler (the bottom of the bowl should not touch the water). Melt the chocolate and butter over medium-low heat, stirring often with a rubber spatula, until completely smooth. Remove from the heat and let cool.

In a separate medium bowl, whisk together the granulated sugar, brown sugar, eggs, and vanilla until smooth. Add the cooled chocolate mixture and whisk to combine.

In a separate small bowl, whisk together the flour, cocoa powder, and salt. Add the flour mixture to the chocolate-egg mixture and combine with a spatula until smooth and uniform. Pour the batter into the prepared baking pan and smooth the top with a spatula.

Dollop the caramel sauce over the top of the brownie batter. Use a butter knife to lightly swirl the caramel into the batter to create a marbleized effect.

Bake for 30 minutes, or until the top looks crisp and cracks begin to form. If a toothpick does not come out perfectly clean when you test the brownies, that is okay. They will set as they cool.

Let cool completely before cutting the brownies into 2-inch squares.

(recipe continues)

SALTED CARAMEL SAUCE

Makes about 1½ cups

1 cup heavy cream
¼ cup granulated sugar
¼ cup packed light brown sugar
4 tablespoons (½ stick) unsalted
   butter
3 tablespoons light corn syrup
¼ teaspoon kosher salt
Seeds from ½ vanilla bean

Combine ½ cup of the cream, the granulated sugar, brown sugar, butter, corn syrup, and salt in an uncovered 1½- or 2-quart heavy-bottomed saucepan and bring to a boil over medium-high heat. Once the sugars have dissolved, whisk the mixture a few times to combine.

Continue to boil the mixture over medium-high heat, whisking occasionally. When deep dark tan bubbles form, the consistency is thick and paste-like, and a candy thermometer reads 250°F, remove from the heat. (This should take about 5 minutes after the mixture reaches a boil.) Do not let the mixture burn.

Add the remaining ½ cup cream and the vanilla bean seeds and whisk to incorporate. Be careful, as the mixture will bubble up and can splatter when the cream is added. Return the saucepan to low heat and bring it to a low boil, whisking vigorously until no visible clumps remain and the caramel sauce is smooth, about 45 seconds.

Immediately pour the hot caramel sauce into a jar or heatproof bowl. Let it cool completely before using.

The caramel sauce will keep in an airtight container in the refrigerator or freezer for at least one month. Gently reheat it to use on ice cream, cake, cookies, or whatever you choose.

GRASSHOPPER SUNDAE
WITH HOMEMADE MARSHMALLOWS

Andrea Reusing

Born in New Orleans in the 1910s, the Grasshopper is a pale green cocktail made of crème de menthe, crème de cacao, and heavy cream. Decades later, it evolved into a chilled pie with a cookie crust, much loved by homemakers like Andrea's grandmother. In tribute, Andrea, the North Carolina chef behind the acclaimed restaurants Lantern and The Durham, has transformed the Grasshopper into a frozen treat with layers of mint ice cream, chocolate sauce, sweet-salty cookie crumbs, crème fraîche whipped cream, and marshmallows. Of course, you can cheat and use store-bought items here, or you can go entirely homemade. Either way, this sophisticated sundae awaits.

Makes 8 sundaes

Chocolate Cookie Crumble

½ cup plus 1 tablespoon all-purpose flour

⅓ cup granulated sugar

3 tablespoons unsweetened cocoa powder

2 teaspoons kosher salt

¼ cup plus 3 tablespoons cold unsalted butter

½ cup finely chopped unsweetened chocolate

Chocolate Sauce

4 ounces dark chocolate, coarsely chopped

1 cup heavy cream

½ cup espresso or strong brewed coffee

¼ cup unsweetened cocoa powder

¼ teaspoon vanilla extract

¼ teaspoon Kosher salt

2 tablespoons crème fraîche

Whipped Crème Fraîche

2 cups crème fraîche

1 teaspoon vanilla extract

1½ tablespoons confectioners' sugar

Fresh Mint Ice Cream (recipe follows) or store-bought

Homemade Marshmallows (recipe follows) or good-quality store-bought marshmallows

Make the cookie crumble: Preheat the oven to 350°F. Line a baking sheet with parchment paper.

In the bowl of a stand mixer fitted with the paddle attachment, or using your hands, mix together the flour, granulated sugar, cocoa powder, salt, and butter until the dough has a grainy, streusel-like texture.

Spread the mixture evenly over the prepared baking sheet and bake until crispy, about 12 minutes. The crumbles will harden more as they cool, so don't worry if they are a little soft in places.

Put the chopped chocolate in a bowl, then add the crumbles on top to melt the chocolate. Mix to combine. Store in a container in the refrigerator until ready to use.

Make the chocolate sauce: Put the chocolate in a medium bowl. In a medium saucepan, whisk together the cream, espresso, and cocoa powder. Bring to a simmer over medium-high heat. Turn off the heat and pour the cream mixture over the chocolate, whisking until the chocolate has melted and the sauce is smooth and glossy. Add the vanilla and salt and stir. Let the sauce cool, then whisk in the 2 tablespoons crème fraîche. Keep warm.

Make the whipped crème fraîche: Just before serving the sundaes, combine the 2 cups crème fraîche, vanilla, and confectioners' sugar in a medium bowl, and whip to soft peaks with a handheld mixer.

Assemble the sundaes: For each sundae, pile three small scoops of the mint ice cream in a bowl or sundae glass and top with the warm chocolate sauce, marshmallows, chocolate cookie crumbles, and whipped crème fraîche.

(recipe continues)

FRESH MINT ICE CREAM

Makes about 2 quarts

3¾ cups whole milk
2½ cups heavy cream
1½ cups packed fresh spearmint
    leaves
1 cup granulated sugar
1 tablespoon corn syrup
¼ cup tapioca starch
¼ teaspoon kosher salt
2 tablespoons crème de menthe

Place the spearmint leaves in a large bowl. In a large saucepan, bring 3½ cups of the milk and the cream to a simmer. Keep an eye on it, as the mixture will boil over easily. Pour the milk mixture over the mint and allow to cool. Once cool, cover with a sheet of plastic wrap, pressing the plastic directly against the surface of the liquid to prevent a skin from forming. Steep for at least 12 hours or overnight.

Strain out the mint and bring the milk mixture to a simmer in a large saucepan. Add the sugar and corn syrup, whisking until the sugar is dissolved. Remove from the heat.

Whisk together the tapioca starch and the remaining ¼ cup milk. Add to the sweetened milk mixture and stir until thickened.

Chill the mixture in an ice water bath, then add the salt and the crème de menthe. Finish in an ice cream maker according to the manufacturer's instructions and store in the freezer until ready to use.

HOMEMADE MARSHMALLOWS

Makes one 8-inch square sheet

Nonstick cooking spray
1 tablespoon plus 1 teaspoon
    unflavored powdered gelatin
¼ cup confectioners' sugar
¼ cup cornstarch
1 vanilla bean
2 cups granulated sugar
3 large egg whites
1½ cups corn syrup

In a small dish, dissolve the gelatin in ¼ cup water. Set aside.

Line a square cake pan or rimmed baking sheet with parchment paper and coat with nonstick spray. Combine the confectioners' sugar and cornstarch and dust the parchment with about half the mixture.

Split the vanilla bean lengthwise and scrape the seeds into a bowl. Add 1 cup of the granulated sugar and toss together.

In a large bowl, using a handheld mixer, whip the egg whites until foamy. Gradually add the remaining 1 cup granulated sugar and whip until the mixture holds soft peaks.

Combine the vanilla sugar and the corn syrup in a medium saucepan and gently stir to combine. Heat over medium-high heat until the syrup registers 240°F on a candy thermometer. Turn off the heat and whisk in the dissolved gelatin, which will be a solid, Jell-O–like piece. Immediately beat the syrup mixture into the egg whites. Try to avoid pouring the syrup directly onto the beaters. Whip until thick and completely cool. It will be very heavy and taffy-like. Spread the marshmallow in the prepared pan.

Dust some of the remaining confectioners' sugar mixture over the marshmallow, saving the excess for later. Chill the marshmallow sheet at least 4 hours or overnight.

Using a pair of oiled scissors, snip the marshmallow sheet into small squares. Dip all sides of the marshmallows into the remaining confectioners' sugar mixture so that there are no exposed sticky surfaces. Store in an airtight container until ready to use.

THE BOMBE

Jeni Britton Bauer

Creamy, coat-your-tongue fromage blanc ice cream is layered with tart ruby-red cherry sorbet to create the classic French dessert known as *la bombe glacée*. As modern as *la bombe* looks, the concept actually dates back a few hundred years. Chefs, in the era when ice cream was mostly reserved for royalty and the rich, would scoop the frozen stuff into molds designed to resemble cannonballs. Today's version is all about peace and love, which is why we asked our girl crush Jeni, the founder of Jeni's Splendid Ice Creams, to create one just for us.

Makes one 9-inch bombe

1 quart Fromage Blanc Ice Cream
   (recipe follows) or store-bought
   buttermilk ice cream
1 quart Cherry Lambic Sorbet
   (recipe follows) or store-bought
   cherry sorbet
Fresh cherries, for serving
Cherry Simple Syrup (recipe follows),
   for serving

Let the fromage blanc ice cream soften. Fill the inside of a 3½-quart metal bowl with the ice cream. Tap the bowl on the counter to remove any air bubbles. Gently insert a smaller 1½-quart metal bowl into the center of the ice cream, wiggling the bowl into place. Don't push it down too far. The rims of the two bowls should be at the same level. Cover the top with plastic wrap and freeze for 4 hours or up to overnight.

Once the ice cream is frozen, remove the smaller bowl by pouring hot tap water into it, being careful not to get water on the ice cream. Let the bowl stand long enough to slightly melt the surrounding ice cream, then remove the inside bowl. Use a spatula to smooth the center. Return the mold to the freezer for at least 1 hour, until frozen firm.

When ready, soften the cherry sorbet. Add the sorbet to the hollow core in your mold. Using an offset spatula, make sure the sorbet is flush with the top rim of the bowl. Tap to remove any air bubbles. Cover with plastic wrap and freeze for 4 hours or up to overnight.

To remove the ice cream from the bowl, dip the bowl into a basin of hot tap water and let sit until the ice cream melts a tiny bit, 15 to 20 seconds. Skim the edge with an offset spatula to loosen. Turn the bowl upside down onto a serving dish and tap to release. Wipe any melted ice cream from the plate and return the bombe to the freezer for 30 minutes or until ready to serve.

To serve, top the bombe with fresh cherries and drizzle with cherry simple syrup.

(recipe continues)

Tip: To mold the sorbet into the ice cream, you will need two metal nesting bowls. When placed inside each other, there should be a minimum of ½ inch of space in between.

FROMAGE BLANC ICE CREAM

Makes 1 generous quart

2 cups whole milk
1 tablespoon plus 1 teaspoon
    cornstarch
½ cup plus 3 tablespoons cream
    cheese, at room temperature
¼ teaspoon kosher salt
1¼ cups heavy cream
⅔ cup granulated sugar
¼ cup light corn syrup

Mix about 2 tablespoons of the milk with the cornstarch in a small bowl to make a smooth slurry.

Whisk the cream cheese and salt in a large bowl until smooth.

Combine the remaining milk with the cream, sugar, and corn syrup in a large saucepan, bring to a rolling boil over medium-high heat, and simmer for 4 minutes. Remove from the heat and gradually whisk in the cornstarch slurry. Bring the mixture back to a boil over medium-high heat and cook, stirring with a wooden spoon, until slightly thickened, about 1 minute. Remove from the heat.

Gradually whisk the hot milk mixture into the cream cheese mixture until smooth. Let cool completely. Cover the bowl and refrigerate for 2 to 3 hours.

Pour the base into your prepared ice cream machine and spin according to the manufacturer's instructions until thick and creamy. Transfer to a container, press a sheet of parchment paper directly on the surface, and seal with an airtight lid. Store in the coldest part of your freezer until firm, at least 4 hours.

CHERRY LAMBIC SORBET

Makes 1 pint

1 pound pitted fresh cherries,
    plus more for garnish
¾ cup granulated sugar
⅓ cup light corn syrup
¾ cup cherry lambic beer, chilled

Purée the cherries in a food processor until smooth. Combine the cherries, sugar, and corn syrup in a medium saucepan and bring to a simmer, stirring to dissolve the sugar. Once dissolved, remove from the heat immediately and let cool. Add the beer, cover the mixture, and refrigerate for 2 to 3 hours.

Pour the base into your prepared ice cream machine and spin according to the manufacturer's instructions until thick and creamy. Stop when the sorbet has the consistency of very softly whipped cream, 30 to 35 minutes.

Pack the sorbet into a container, press a sheet of parchment paper directly on the surface, and seal with an airtight lid. Store in the coldest part of your freezer until firm, at least 4 hours.

CHERRY SIMPLE SYRUP

Makes about 1¾ cups

1¼ cups granulated sugar
10 cherries

Place the sugar, cherries, and 1 cup water in a saucepan over medium heat. Simmer until the sugar has dissolved completely and the cherries soften and begin to break down, about 5 minutes. Strain out the cherries and discard. Let the syrup cool completely, then refrigerate in a covered container for up to 1 week. Use for The Bombe or use to flavor lemonade, seltzer, or other drinks.

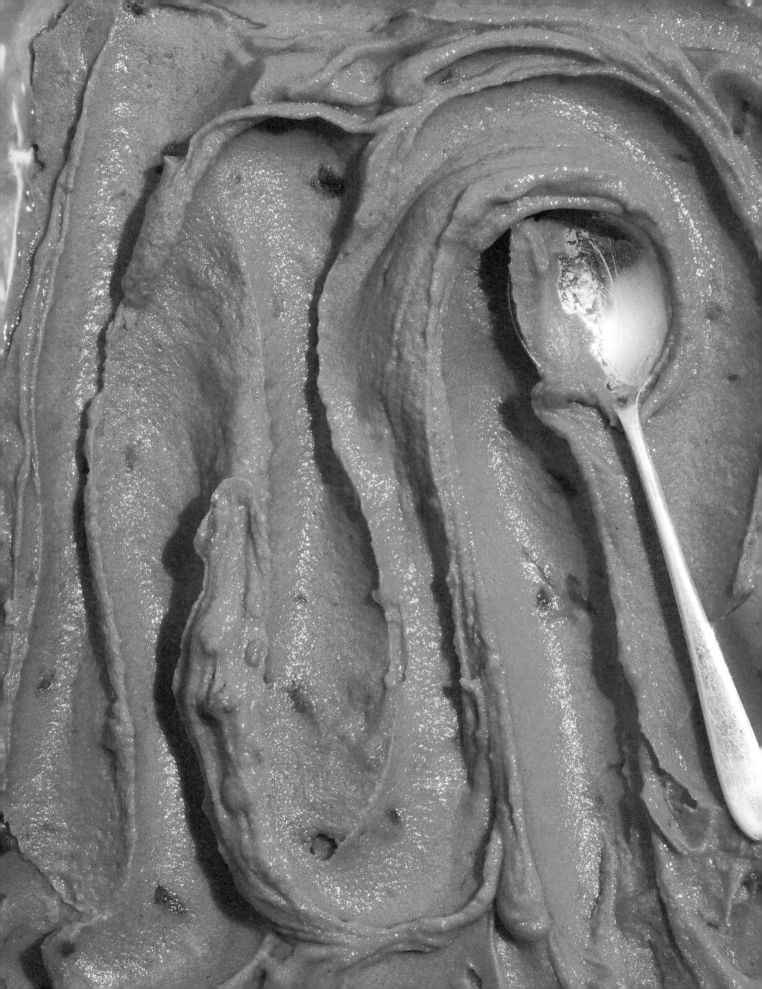

ACKNOWLEDGMENTS

Kerry & Claudia would like to thank:

• All the amazing women who let us share their stories and recipes in these pages.

• The dream team that helped make this book a reality: Alpha Smoot, Claudia Ficca, Diana Yen, Katja Greeff, and Cindi Gasparre.

• Donna Yen and Kate Miller Spencer. You two are the Bombe.

• Alexandria Misch, Gillie Houston, Annabel Surtees, Gabi Vigoreaux, and Lauren Salkeld, for helping with all the nitty-gritty stuff and extra chores that go into making a cookbook.

• Byrne Fahey, for cooking your heart out all summer.

• The rock star assistants on the photo shoot: Dayna Seman, Anna Neidermeyer, Michelle Longo, Britta Siddell, Kyle Acebo, Jessica Leibowitz, and Chelsie Craig.

• Andy McNicol, agent extraordinaire. We're glad we bumped into you at that Thakoon dinner.

• The whole team at Clarkson Potter: Aaron Wehner, Doris Cooper, Angelin Borsics, Ashley Meyer, Rica Allannic, Stephanie Huntwork, Kate Tyler, Stephanie Davis, Natasha Martin, Heather Williamson, and Amy Boorstein. Thank you for believing in us and in so many female authors.

• Our families, friends, and Chef Rob Newton.

• Our Kickstarter supporters, all of our past interns, the crew at Heritage Radio Network, the tireless Jennifer Livingston, and all of our wonderful stockists.

• Jean Armstrong and the team at Williams-Sonoma.

• The talented ceramists who lent us their beautiful plates, platters, and glasses: MONDAYS, Henry Street Studio, Noble Plateware, Amelia Black Ceramics, and Mud Australia.

• The lovely folks at Staub, KitchenAid, Le Creuset, and The French Farm.

• All the indie shopkeepers who didn't know they were helping but did, including Caputo's, A Cook's Companion, Sahadi's, Kalustyan's, Dual Specialty Store, and Sue and Joe at Santo's Farm. Also, the crew at thekitchn.com for knowing what advice we needed before we did.

• And last but not least, the Bombe Squad. Thank you for all your support and sisterhood.

INDEX

Note: Page references in *italics* indicate photographs.